There's a Government in Your Soup

There's a Government in Your Soup

◆

Why There's Too Much Government in Your Kitchen, and What You Can Do About It

Brad Edmonds

iUniverse, Inc.
New York Lincoln Shanghai

There's a Government in Your Soup
Why There's Too Much Government in Your Kitchen, and What You Can Do About It

iUniverse, Inc.

For information address:
iUniverse, Inc.
2021 Pine Lake Road, Suite 100
Lincoln, NE 68512
www.iuniverse.com

ISBN: 0-595-31816-9

Printed in the United States of America

Contents

Introduction

Everybody loves food. Everybody knows everybody loves food. What isn't well known is how much more we might love it—how much safer, less expensive, and more varied it could be—in the absence of meddlesome government interventions. My purpose in writing this book is to show how government meddling works; how it hampers our enjoyment and liberties; and how we might lessen government's intrusions into our kitchens and lives.

How did I come to write about this? I dreamed of writing a book for years, as nearly all of us have; and as nearly all of us do, I gradually forgot that dream in the face of the workaday realities of a full-time job, tending to a house, and keeping up with too many extracurricular activities. I still made time for writing, but never dared to expect more than getting the occasional freelance article published.

And then I found my niche: Finding things we all share and enjoy, and writing about how government mucks them up, and how freely-acting individuals make them beautiful in spite of it. Food does a better job than just about anything else of exemplifying the problems with over-regulation. Enough people told me that I should write a book that I finally set out to realizing an almost-forgotten dream.

In this book, I show the expanding and sometimes invisible reach of government into every aspect of life. I also show some of the beauty and ingenuity of free minds working within (relatively) free markets. Criticizing government by finding specific problems is easy, since government has gotten so big, and many authors who criticize government are themselves criticized for failing to offer alternatives. Thus, I conclude by discussing the ways we can act to scale back government to more sane levels, both locally and nationally.

What standing do I have to write such a book? I've been employed in the public sector—in universities as a graduate assistant, graduate fellow, and teacher; and in Washington, DC as an operations trainee with CIA. I've seen some of the government from the inside. I've also been a church administrator, banker, and retail manager, so I've seen government from the outside as well. Too many years of school resulted in Master's degrees in business and psychology, a Doctorate in music, and an embarrassing collection of cookbooks. Finally, I've written for a few prominent websites—LewRockwell.com and the site of the Ludwig von Mises Institute, www.Mises.org—for a few years, and have had a chance to learn from and debate with some strong economic minds. More than anything else, I've learned how to learn.

And since I love to laugh, eat, and generally have a good time, I love to see other folks having a good time. If you don't have a good time, you won't keep reading, so this book is not a long, bitter, anti-government rant. I let myself have fun all the way through. And finally, I'm accessible: If you have any questions, would like some documentation, or just want to disagree, you can write me at governmentinyoursoup@yahoo.com. Cheers!

Acknowledgements

No man is an island, and no book owes exclusively to the efforts of its author. My parents and numerous friends have provided encouragement beyond the call of duty; my parents went even farther by putting up with my seemingly endless years of graduate school. The Ludwig von Mises Institute has given me freelance editing opportunities that developed skills helpful in writing my own book. And Lew Rockwell, founder and president of the Mises Institute, gave me the first and still best opportunity I have to make my views public. I hoist a cold one in appreciation to all of them, and dedicate my efforts to justifying their confidence.

1

Food Ideology?

The United States is one of the freest nations in the world. Even so, if you live here there is pretty much nothing you can do, from the time you get up in the morning to the time you go to bed, that isn't touched by government. Even sleep itself must be on a government-tested and -approved mattress, with a materials-disclosure tag which, under penalty of law, can't be removed before the final consumer purchases it. This is because the government wants the final consumer to receive flame-resistance information, and the government doesn't trust you, the consumer, to look for such information. Nor does government trust the manufacturer to provide information without a government regulation being imposed. Everything you can buy and almost everything you can do is touched by government.

No part of life exemplifies the nannying, grasping, expansive, sometimes self-contradictory nature of government better than the world of food. Food, in its history, production, and preparation, can illustrate much of what can be said about the problems with our expanding government—a government that often functions at the whim of special interests—and about the far-reaching, color-blind benefits of free markets and free people. Food history teaches not only that governmental fiddling with the economy needlessly makes life worse for consumers, but also that private organizations can do the things government has taken over. One need look no further than tea for both of these lessons, as I will show later on.

A comical example of government meddling: Early in the year 2001, the US government made it difficult for plum growers to package their dried plums under the name "dried plums." Plum growers wanted to distance their product from the negative connotations that have come to be associated with the word "prune." The government resisted the "new" term, reminding us that government sometimes will bend over backwards to make peaceful, voluntary transactions difficult for people who actually produce food for sale, as it will for people

1

who produce, buy, and sell everything else. The fact that government trusts only itself to inspect meat, while we have frequent E. coli scares and meat recalls, shows that we shouldn't trust government meddling even when it is advertised as being benign and protective of our interests.

As to the universal benefits of free markets and free people, the food speaks for itself. We have developed chickens and turkeys so bloated with flesh they can barely walk. Instead of walking, they're providing mountains of inexpensive, nutritious, low-fat protein. We have developed numerous varieties of cabbage that never would have developed in nature (how many plants produce their main bulk in leaves that are never exposed to the sun?). All our fruits and vegetables are far more tasty and/or presentable than nature was making them just a few hundred—or few dozen—years ago. And we've begun producing such things as precooked bacon that keeps for months without refrigeration, and nutritious diet meals in a can. Further, after drinking all the great coffee and tea we can find, we can buy little strips of plastic that make our teeth whiter. Five years ago we had to pay our dentists hundreds of dollars for the same results we get now for $22 from an aisle in Wal-Mart.

Finally, the tremendous variety and affordability of our food, even in the face of government interventions, exemplifies the naturally peaceful, productive, and creative character that a free society always develops. In a truly free society, all transactions are voluntary—none are coerced. When transactions are voluntary, you as the seller must provide a product or service that makes your customer leave the transaction feeling better off than when he entered it.

We are indeed free to buy or not buy a tomato under today's circumstances, but the heavy hand of government makes that tomato perhaps twice as expensive as it would be if the tomato grower, your grocer, and you were all left alone. As we'll see later on, the tomato grower is not free to produce his tomatoes in the most efficient way he can think of; the grocer is not allowed to run his store in the most efficient way he can think of; and you're not allowed to earn your money, drive to the store, and buy the tomato as efficiently as possible.

When our country was created, the founding fathers had a clear vision. The central government was strictly limited to a few specific missions, and state governments were allowed to govern however their citizens wanted (as long as they didn't institute royalty). There was no income tax, there were no rules governing how you used your own property, and there was no one telling farmers how much they could grow, where they could grow it, or when they would be allowed to grow it.

The freedom our founders envisioned is rapidly eroding. Government, at every level, now has the power to decide what you can do with your property. The intrusion can range from merely taxing you for having the audacity to own property, to forcing you to leave your property "natural" to protect an endangered bug or rodent. Indeed, you can have your property taken away if someone with more political clout than you—say, a mall developer—decides he wants it, and your city council decides they want him to have your property. This is what results when government is allowed to decide for itself the extent of its own powers.

But even under our present circumstances, there is some liberty remaining with regard to food. You can grow vegetables, at least; and you can keep some small animals and bugs (!)—more about that later—as livestock. In a limited way, you can cross-breed, cross-fertilize, and develop your own favorite foods, as long as you don't dare try to sell them. Food remains the only thing you can produce efficiently at home without government oversight and without paying taxes on either production or consumption.

This extends even to alcoholic beverages, though there are limits to how much booze you can produce at home without having to subject yourself to licensing and inspections. Anything else you could produce at home—clothing or furniture, for example—is being produced so efficiently by the market that you could not produce it yourself without spending more money and time than it's worth, unless you're a hobbyist and do it for enjoyment. Even then, you're taxed on the raw materials. With food, once you have seeds (or a pair of rabbits), you're done with government meddling.

Hence, food provides a rich and bottomless source of examples that teach lessons about politics, culture, economics, and history. Each food item at your grocery store owes its appearance and flavor to the ingenuity of ancient cultures and modern entrepreneurs and scientists alike, and much of its price to all manner of government intervention that can take the form of taxes, regulations, and price supports that raise your cost merely because some politicians of the distant past wanted to buy more votes from farmers, and those politicians were willing to do it by gouging the rest of us.

The cultural lessons are equally interesting. As an example, there may be a reason why traditional southern food is spicy, meaty, nutritious, and satisfying, yet southerners themselves are religious, mannerly, and reserved; while much the opposite holds for northern food and northerners (in general, of course; present readers excepted). There may be a reason why Italy has produced the finest and most varied cuisine in the world—this, even though it is a tiny nation character-ized by political and technological buffoonery for most of the last 2,000 years.

In this book, I use as examples everything from specific food ingredients to recipes to national cuisines to show how government intervention is always prob-lematic, resulting in reduced variety, higher prices, and even reduced safety for consumers; and how economic freedom benefits all participants in a mar-ket—every producer and every consumer.

2

There's a Government in Your Soup

Government regulations are everywhere, sapping our productivity while providing additional power for elected officials without guaranteeing an abundant, safe, affordable food supply. There may have been times when it seemed government should get involved with the food supply: During the Great Depression, during WWII, during severe droughts, and so on. But in all these cases, allowing free markets and free trade would have lessened or completely prevented the problems that arose.

For example, during the Dust Bowl era, our drought was not worldwide, but food production was. Tea, as we'll see later, was first imported to Europe from China 500 years ago, so importing food would have been no problem 75 years ago. But to the contrary, during the Dust Bowl drought, we were in the Great Depression, when trade protectionism was at an historic high in our history (meaning free trade was at an historic low).

But free trade and abundant supplies are only part of the equation. Our government tries to guarantee a safe food supply by providing mandatory inspections and state and federal approval of certain foods and producers. Unfortunately, government officials don't have enough incentive to do a good job. When's the last time a government agency went out of business for failing to ensure a safe food supply? It'll never happen. No government agencies went out of business when people started getting sickened and killed by E. coli in the 1990s. Instead, the government agencies forced businesses to spend millions of dollars putting safe-handling labels on various types of food, beginning with raw (and sometimes fully cooked) meats.

Today, government action guarantees nothing but higher prices and *less* abundant supply; but if private businesses were in charge of food safety—businesses that could easily go bankrupt with a little bad publicity following a failure—our food supply would certainly be safer as well. Take a look at the track record of *Consumer Reports* to get an idea of how trustworthy a private enterprise can be when it enters the consumer-protection arena. Let's get a look at how government regulations really function:

HOW GOVERNMENT REGULATIONS COST YOU MONEY

In the case of Nix vs. Hedden, argued before the United States Supreme Court in 1893, it was determined for all Americans for all time that the tomato is a vegetable. The Court decided that although dictionary and botanical definitions of "fruit" and "vegetable" suggested the tomato properly should be considered a fruit, it would thereafter be considered a vegetable nonetheless. The suit appears to have been brought because there were import taxes on vegetables at the time, while no such taxes existed to discourage the importation of fruits; more about that in a minute.

Which is the tomato, really? Botanically, it is a fruit: There's a fleshy part surrounding the seeds, and that's the part we eat. Apples, oranges, cucumbers, squash, and bean pods thus fit the definition of fruit. Most fruits are sweet so animals will eat them and spread the seeds. By contrast, vegetables—leaves, stalks, roots—are things the plants need for their own nutrition. The plants don't want those eaten by critters, so they're less sweet. Horticulturally, however, the tomato plant is a vegetable plant: There is no woody trunk, as fruit plants have.

The Supreme Court also took into consideration, perhaps making it the primary consideration, that most fruits are eaten for dessert, while most vegetables are eaten with an earlier meal course. The Court therefore decided there was enough evidence to declare however they wanted for the hapless plant, so they declared however they wanted. (Most of the "evidence" reviewed in the case: dictionary definitions.)

Thus, in 1893, we had private vegetable growers gorging themselves at the trough of government handouts. They were hoping to gain a windfall in the form of protection against foreign competition. Foreign tomatoes, upon being declared vegetables, were then subject to import taxes. They thus became more expensive, so domestic producers could raise their own prices. (By analogy, in the 1980s, American auto manufacturers raised minivan prices by $2,000 when new US import tariffs of $2000 were enacted.) Additionally, by changing the classification of the innocent tomato from a food not taxed to one taxed as a result of Nix vs. Hedden, the government provided itself a little extra money where none had been before.

Who pays the higher prices for domestic food, and the taxes on imported food? You do, of course. Who benefits? Aside from government, the beneficiaries are those people in those industries who can get the government to impose the taxes. Once the taxes are imposed, you are stuck with them. The government has legal authority to impose these taxes and demand you pay them on threat of violence—fines, imprisonment, confiscation of possessions, all enforced at gunpoint. So we have higher-priced tomatoes for the benefit of a grasping government and a few American tomato producers. Bon appetit!

It's interesting to compare this to the case with prunes, mentioned earlier. Prunes are dried plums, of course, but plum growers had to get FDA approval to change the old and tired name, "prune," to the more descriptive and marketable "dried plum." The FDA in fact prohibited plum growers from labeling prune juice "dried plum juice," calling it a contradiction in terms that would be confusing to us poor, stupid consumers (though we already know the contradiction is in terms only or there wouldn't be juice at all).

What we see, then, is a government that is pleased to overrule scientists in classifying plant life if there's money in it for the government, or the favor of a large voting bloc. At the same time, this government is loath to allow a simple name change from one valid name to another if there's nothing in it for the government. In the dried plum squabble the government claimed it was attempting to protect the consumer from confusion, but note that the government has no interest in protecting the consumer from artificially high prices.

Government employees and appointed and elected officials are ordinary people, and perfectly capable of succumbing to the temptation to benefit themselves at your expense. Private businessmen can be this way, too, and they are only too happy to lobby the government to make laws that benefit them, again at your expense. The way to keep businessmen perfectly honest is to make them compete with each other. Take away from them the juicy prize of governmental shackles on their competitors, and you benefit. As just one mechanism, businesses would spend less time and money lobbying the government for protections (often, nowadays, these protections are from government itself). The savings would be passed on to you. Many of the businessmen would benefit, too, by the way: In your business, would the absence of government red tape make it easier, or more difficult, to focus on satisfying the customer?

And notice the amazing behaviors exhibited by government employees. Supreme Court justices were willing to take biology into their own hands to settle a taxation question, when virtually the only evidence presented was read from dictionaries, and none of the judges was a botanical expert. Whenever someone has no competition for his job, little possibility of misbehaving so badly he might lose his job, and the power of legal coercion to enforce his will, he can be expected to make nonsensical decisions.

HOW GOVERNMENT REGULATIONS HURT AMERICAN BUSINESSES

We know government regulation can "help" American businesses by putting shackles on their foreign competition. Tariffs—basically, taxes you pay our government for the luxury of buying a foreign product—are meant to protect domestic industry from foreign competition. As our own auto industry shows, what tariffs really do is allow domestic industries to raise the prices they charge you and me, without improving quality. One result of tariffs is that American cars are as expensive as Japanese cars without being nearly as good—check any JD Power auto quality data to confirm this. Put another way, tariffs swath domestic businessmen in the luxury of not having to be as good as foreign businessmen when competing for the American consumer's dollar. Is it any wonder that the Honda Accord and Toyota Camry outsell the Ford Taurus and Chevrolet Impala year after year?

What is less well-known is that government regulations other than tariffs can directly threaten domestic industries. Often, these regulations are written with heartwarming, big-brotherly intent; just as often, they are unnecessary and expensive, and do more harm than good. One example is the apple industry. I interviewed an apple grower from the state of Washington, and he told me the following:

American apple growers generally are losing money right now. One of the biggest single demands on the growers' time is "keeping legal" (alas, they even have a jargon for it). For example, they have to submit forms to the government demonstrating that they have provided approved training for the wearing of goggles, the use of ladders, and tractor operation. A decent businessman in the apple business might employ 60 people in season, many of them migrants. That's a lot of training sessions, with forms to be filled out later.

How many of us need eyewear or ladder training, particularly since ladders already have government-mandated decals showing how to use them properly? How many farmers, with or without a government mandate, will put a new employee on a $200,000 tractor without showing him how to operate it? (I worked on a farm one summer while in college, and the farm owner wouldn't let me touch a tractor without him checking me out on it first, and that was when there were no forms to fill out.) And will the government understand how to do this training better than an individual farmer, training a particular employee to use a particular tractor?

The government apparently assumes apple growers are stupid. The chemicals sprayed on the apples are so thoroughly tested and so safe, my apple grower's adult son sometimes will pull an apple off a tree and eat it a few days after spraying…and yet the government mandates that nobody can even enter the orchard for several days after spraying with certain chemicals, as if the apple growers don't read labels or can't understand them. My interviewee's house is in the orchard. Should he go to a hotel every time he sprays? Knowing the apple growers are morons, the government decides what chemicals they can use.

Maybe the government doesn't know that on their own, for the last 20 years, the growers have been hiring consultants to keep "good" and "bad" bugs in balance; the bugs take care of each other. Apple growers use fewer pesticides that way, and they didn't need a government mandate to start managing the bugs. They just needed the profit motive, and the motive provided by a free market in personal-injury lawyering.

There are apple growers I'd call stupid, by the way—hippies who grow organically. Some of the commercial farmers are growing organically, and they're having to apply "natural" pesticides and fertilizers constantly to approach the productivity of "inorganic" (?) farms. Some of the hippies are using cow manure. They pick the food off the ground. Thus, mainly "organic" apples are likely to be contaminated with E. coli bacteria, and once contaminated, some produce is impossible to sanitize.[1] The apples being sprayed by chemicals known to be safe for wildlife and people, chemicals costing up to $700 per gallon, have never poisoned any customers. But they're the apples the environmentalists want to ban in favor of organic apples that are more likely to be contaminated by cow poop laden with bacteria that can kill children.

While the government assumes the actual apple growers are stupid, the government follows the advice of some inexpert people who really *are* stupid. Meryl Streep had the ear of our national government years ago when she referred to Alar

---

1.   See Solomon, E. B., Yaron, S., and Matthews, K. R. (2002), Transmission of Escherichia coli O157:H7 from Contaminated Manure and Irrigation Water to Lettuce Plant Tissue and Its Subsequent Internalization, *Applied and Environmental Microbiology*, 68:397–400.

as a poisonous pesticide (two lies in one—it was a growth regulator that kept apples from falling off trees too soon, and it dissipated long before apples got to market, so it wasn't even poisonous), and yet Meryl Streep herself, when invited by the apple industry to visit and learn the real facts, refused the invitation. Alar was a great product; we now have fewer apples at higher cost without it.

The results of this government involvement in private industry are far-reaching. American apple growers are closing up shop, while foreign apples are the only thing in my store-brand apple juice. You may remember, when stumping during the 2000 presidential campaign, the economic genius Al Gore telling a group of the Future Farmers of America that they should find another career because America can't do it as inexpensively as other countries. Some of the apples in the juice in my fridge are from Germany. I thought Germany was pretty fully developed, and in fact thoroughly socialist, and therefore less efficient, than the United States; why should their apples be cheaper than ours? But they are, so Al Gore was right, and the load of regulations foisted on our apple growers are the reason he was right.

Any government involvement in any private industry is going to do damage. Corporate welfare and strangling regulations meant to save trees and mice and people from the actions of other people have two reliable results: the wasting of our industry, by making it too profitable, hence fat and lazy, or in other cases not profitable enough; and some version of the opposite of the desired effect, either in hurting our industries or poisoning us. I have nothing against imports, and the American market is starving for imported apples and steel, but let it be exclusively because someone else innovated—meaning we can innovate right back at them—and not just because our government stepped in and mucked everything up.

GOVERNMENT REGULATIONS AND FOOD SAFETY

It made news in the summer of 2001 when the FDA decided to get into the act of telling us how we should and should not eat eggs. The FDA mandated that safe-handling and -preparation instructions be added to egg cartons, costing the industry millions of dollars that are passed on to us in the form of higher prices. Let's back up a bit, and look at the government's food-safety record.

One of my favorite restaurants has this message on the menu: "It is a Florida state law that all burgers be grilled to medium temperature. If you insist, we'll break that law." Their burgers are 12 ounces of beef, the best I've ever had, ground by the restaurant from their own Angus steak trimmings. They're the only restaurant burgers I'll trust to eat undercooked, and they're always perfect and succulent. In Alabama, my local county health department considers it a violation of law if a restaurateur serves ground beef with any pink showing on the inside. As is probably the case in Florida, my health department will ignore the infraction if the customer has made clear in his order that he wants it less than fully cooked.

E. coli, a fecal bacterium that may contaminate beef, is nothing to sneer at. It'll hurt you and it can kill a child or elderly person. As I understand it, the bacterium hadn't been found often in beef before 1980, though it was identified in the human colon as far back as 1885. It came to the forefront of national consciousness in 1993 when a Jack in the Box fast food restaurant in the state of Washington sickened some 700 customers, killing four. No one pointed out at the time that the meat was USDA inspected and approved.

Likewise, a more recent episode involved a Canadian public water supply; in this case, authorities *knew* the water purification system wasn't working properly. They let it go for long enough to result in the deaths of at least seven people.[2] As for us in the US, remember that every recall of contaminated beef has been for beef inspected and approved by the USDA.

Compare such episodes with New York City. The city government ensures that food labeled "kosher" is indeed kosher for observant Jews—as though the city has any business doing this. The Jews in New York ignore the city stamp, and look for a rabbi's stamp. The rabbis' standards are higher. People are right to be suspicious of the city's approval—government employees face the wrong incentives to be trusted with food safety. I haven't heard of government inspectors facing recrimination in the event of an E. coli outbreak.

The rabbi, on the other hand, faces the right incentives, and takes food safety seriously. No rabbi would want his flock to violate scriptural commands; nor would he want to risk his own credibility. Per the 14th amendment's (supposed) extension of the Bill of Rights to state governments, the 1st amendment says the New York City government has no business telling Jews whether they are properly observant of the Torah; and no individual city employee's credibility is at risk if non-kosher food is labeled "kosher" in error.

---

2.   Recounted at http://cnews.canoe.ca/CNEWS/Canada/2003/04/23/71610-cp.html, accessed May, 2004.

While in college, I worked at a 24-hour breakfast restaurant. The restaurant scored an 85 out of 100 from the county health department. In that county, 85 is a high enough score to stay in business, but not great for the restaurant's public image. The same restaurant was scored in the low 70s by their own corporate office's private inspectors. According to the inspection score sheet, such a score was unsatisfactory and seemed to constitute a threat to the manager's job, according to the handwritten rant on the margin of the inspection checklist.

In the same county, I knew of one restaurant that got a 99 instead of 100 because sugar was in a container labeled "cinnamon." In another county in Alabama, a restaurant lost two points off its health rating for a stained ceiling tile in the restaurant foyer. That restaurant owner doesn't eat at other restaurants unless he's allowed to look over the kitchen, and I know his own kitchen is immaculate. I'll always feel safe eating at his restaurant, regardless what the county inspector says.

The funny thing is, the government that requires all the inspections, the government that wants to determine how much we cook our own beef and eggs at home, is the same government whose consistent unreliability is the worst food-safety risk around. Without government inspections, we likely would handle our food more carefully at home and pay more attention to appearance and odor in stores, as we did before the nanny state took the responsibility upon itself. The government's assurance that a given food is safe probably does more harm than good.

Without government inspections and government criteria, we wouldn't have so many large producers (apparently) striving to meet only the government's mandated minimum levels of purity, with occasional tragic results. I would like the option of choosing between beef producers who have their own standards of cleanliness. There is no doubt that some would be supremely reliable. Then, I wouldn't have to eat dry, overcooked hamburgers every time. I'd pull out the classical beef tartar recipes.

And for people who can't tell when a piece of meat is safe (indeed, I'm sure I couldn't tell whether a piece of meat is contaminated with E. coli), there would arise private consumer-protection outfits. The best grocery stores would have meat with the "Good Meatkeeping" seal of approval, and this meat would cost perhaps 25 cents per pound more than other beef. And you can bet the inspectors at Good Meatkeeping would do serious work—more like the rabbis than the government inspectors. You can buy a blind eye from a government inspector with a bribe; he loses nothing if a few children die. A rabbi or a professional private inspector loses his job and faces lawsuits if he's wrong.

None of this should be surprising. As with Social Security, Corporate Average Fuel Economy requirements, anything having to do with the environment, and anything else into which the government has put its paws, the process is the same: Government perceives a need (because the market has first identified it); government steps in to help; government ends up making everything worse by selecting a single solution, forcing all of us to abide by it, and by enforcing it with employees who aren't held fully accountable.

GOVERNMENT AND FOOD PRICES

Find somebody who was at least a teenager during the Great Depression, and watch him eat. He won't want to leave a morsel on the plate. This is true of any American who lived through WWII, when food was rationed by the government as it is in Cuba today. During more than a decade of their lives, Americans of the 1930s and '40s endured scarcity in food—something we haven't experienced since, and which hasn't arisen without the help of government in any country in generations.

These people clean their plates because, remembering a time when everything on the plate wasn't always enough, they feel moral pangs at the thought of letting food go to waste. This applies even to their children and grandchildren: My parents still retain a heartfelt abhorrence of waste, as was often expressed at dinnertime during my childhood.

But abundance isn't enough for some folks. If you can afford to lobby persistently and stridently before Congress, you can turn abundance into scarcity, plenty into want, and create misfortune for others for your benefit. It takes only a vote on Capitol Hill. Consider the following, from a news item carried by CNN in early 2002: "There's such a glut of prunes that the department is paying growers to destroy 20,000 acres of plum trees. USDA also has been paying farmers to destroy potato and sugar crops, and last year sharply restricted the amount of cranberries that could be brought to market."

I want to say that one more time: The government is paying farmers to destroy thousands of acres of plum trees, potato crops, and sugar crops; and is telling farmers how many cranberries they can sell, and telling you how many you can buy. Imagine what your parents or grandparents would say upon hearing such news. They would consider it a crime, if people anywhere in the world are starving, to burn fruit trees that could produce for years to come. Yes, I realize farm subsidies are common knowledge; heck, even the otherwise principled and estimable Alan Keyes buys into them, as his website declared when he was competing for the 2000 Republican presidential nomination. How could he not, with so many votes at stake?

But the real meaning and import of farm subsidies has nothing to do with people starving. It is merely the forced redistribution of wealth from you and me to a loud special-interest group—farmers—and a transfer of power to the elected policymakers who oversee the process. Not only are we taxed to provide the money to pay the farmers to destroy their crops, but the whole reason for destroying the crops is to keep our prices higher by artificially restricting supply. Thus, we're paying twice for this price-support system that does nothing but destroy wealth for all of us except a few farmers and their benefactors in Washington.

We would be outraged if the government paid Ford to destroy 20,000 new cars in order to keep prices higher (too bad we're not equally outraged at the tariffs that serve as price supports for Ford, GM, and Chrysler). You would be enraged if the government paid your insurance company to burn some of its emergency-reserve cash holdings. We ought to be just as outraged that the government continues to waste our paychecks in the process of making sure that the dollars we earn and are allowed to keep will buy us less food. And it keeps getting ridiculouser: It hit the network news (e.g., ABC's 20/20, October 18, 2002) that some of the windfall from suing tobacco companies has been used by states to subsidize new tobacco production facilities. This proves beyond a shadow of a doubt that the tobacco lawsuits weren't about public health or about tobacco companies lying about the dangers of smoking; the lawsuits were really only about revenue for the states.

Moving to free markets in food (and health care, and energy, and so on) might shock a few producers at first. Some farmers would have to find other work, or work their farms as contractors for larger agribusinesses. Such is the march of progress, and it can be only good news that fewer and fewer people would have to labor to provide the market with basic necessities. The benefits for all of us, both immediate and long term, would be lower prices and more abundant supplies of everything edible.

TAXES AND FOOD

It would be impossible to compute the percentage of the price you pay for food that goes to taxes. It will vary with the food item and with the city, county, and state you live in. But we know it's at least criminally burdensome when we look over the process of commercial food production.

The taxation begins with everything that precedes food production that isn't itself food. Farmers pay taxes on water, land, equipment, and supplies. The people who produced all these things the farmer needs—people like Caterpillar and Monsanto—paid their own taxes on their own supplies, labor, transportation, and everything else. Then the farmer has to pay the government for the privilege of producing the food—payroll taxes, social security, and so on; as do canneries, packing houses, and your local grocery store.

Then there are transportation taxes in moving the food from wherever it is produced to wherever it is packaged, and taxes again on moving it to your grocery store. You've probably seen an 18-wheeler with a sign on the back saying the owner pays around $5,000 per year per truck in road-use taxes. And the road-use taxes probably have the smallest impact of all the taxes that end up in the price of the product. Then you finally pay sales taxes at the end of all that; and you're paying the sales taxes out of your paycheck, which has already been taxed.

There are some points along the chain of events from production to consumption—known as the "value chain" in business-school textbooks—where sales taxes are not paid. For example, in Alabama, if you are buying certain products expressly for resale, you avoid local sales taxes. Still, by the time everything above is considered, the true portion of your food prices that owe to taxes alone is onerous; I remember seeing estimates in the 40% range, but again, localities and foods will vary, and a reliable estimate might be impossible to obtain. The full effect of government is worse than the taxes alone, however: Remember that subsidies, tariffs, and other price supports (such as the orchard burnings) drive our prices up even more.

If we're going to have a government, we must have taxes. Note, however, that the money you are coerced to pay in taxation often supports causes you disagree with. If you are an avid pro-lifer, you would be offended to know that some of your tax money has been used to support abortion clinics in the US and overseas. If you are staunchly pro-choice, on the other hand, you might be offended to know that in Alabama, some of our tax money supports the option motorists have to buy a pro-life license plate. Many Christians believe in the New Testament dictum that someone who doesn't work shouldn't eat (see II Thessalonians, for example), but many government social programs for which we are forced to pay give away food stamps, paychecks, medical benefits, and more to people who scam the system, preferring simply not to work. Democrats and Republicans alike are forced to pay taxes on milk and bread, taxes that support government activity Democrats and Republicans consider immoral.

Would you rather give voluntarily to support programs and services you agree with, while paying half as much for food? That's what a free market would provide.

What can you do about it? There are a few things, and I cover them in more detail at the end of this book. Voting exclusively for politicians who want to lower taxes would be a start, but don't expect it to have a profound effect during your lifetime. Politicians almost never have a strong incentive to cut taxes. Reducing taxes, reducing government handout programs, and reducing the size of government and its intrusions into our daily lives would reduce the power of individual politicians, and it would be unnatural for any politician to want that. You can relocate to another state, however—the French provide an amusing example of tax-avoiding relocation, from a few hundred years before the socialist French Revolution:

The word "troglodyte," as far as we know, comes from ancient Greek, perhaps in its origin meaning those who enter holes. It came to refer to a mythical or ancient race of people who lived in caves. Around the 15th century in France, the term came into common use to refer to a group of political activists who found their way around property taxes.

While there is little information available about them, we know there were certain rebels in France who decided to live in caves. Property taxes were assessed in such a way that people living underground avoided the taxes. Entire neighborhoods, complete with restaurants, sprouted in hillsides and mountainsides. There are still villages in France, in the Loire Valley, that offer tours of the underground communities. If it were so easy to avoid property taxes today, you can be sure that the current migration from the northeastern US to the southeast would be supplanted by a migration to the Rockies and Appalachians.

Today, the term "troglodyte" has an exclusively negative connotation. Computer geeks use it to deride "hackers who never leave their cubicles" (according to an online dictionary), while the rest of us use it to deride anyone suspicious or ignorant of the latest technology. It would be in character for me to suggest that a negative connotation of the term developed in France when the troglodytes were living in their caves—perhaps the government put the term into circulation to make tax protestors seem ridiculous—but as far as I could find, there is no reason to assume the term was anything but descriptive. Etymology suggests it was a fitting term, useful to denote cave dwellers but not carrying any particular political meaning.

How can we be troglodytes today? Buy property in Alabama, which has the lowest property taxes in the nation; or buy property offshore. Otherwise, there aren't many effective tax-avoidance strategies available to us. You may have heard of those folks who have hired lawyers to keep the IRS at bay while they pay no income taxes, but this strategy doesn't seem terribly efficient, even if you win.

The Amish provide another sort of example. Traditionally, the Amish have educated their children themselves, and only through the 8th grade (but, and trust me on this, don't get yourself into a math, spelling, or geography bee with an Amish 8th-grader if you don't want to be embarrassed). In 1968, Wisconsin decided to force Amish residents to formally educate their children through the 12th grade. Kansas, Ohio, and Pennsylvania already had successfully defeated the Amish on this front, but some Amish in Wisconsin decided to fight, taking the case to the United States Supreme Court by 1972, in the famous case of Wisconsin v. Yoder. This was a risky move for the Amish: Before, they would simply move to another state when life became intolerable (something our founders had in mind, actually, when they invented our federalist political structure). Setting the wrong precedent in the Supreme Court would consolidate power against the Amish in all 50 states, meaning they would lose hope of retaining their communal sovereignty. Many would no doubt feel compelled to leave the country.

The Supreme Court ruled in their favor, however, and the Amish retained their freedom. Using similar strategies, the Amish have won some exemptions from social security, Medicare, and Medicaid taxes. They have argued successfully that care of the elderly is a family and community responsibility, and that government medical insurance suggests a reliance on someone or something other than God and hard work. They'll have no part of any government insurance. One might assume the Amish don't use hospitals and doctors anyway, but this is a myth. They just pay as they go. If the patient can't afford the bill, members of the community with more resources will help. Note that in this "communist" system, they don't lose any of the money to bureaucratic overhead—100% goes to the beneficiary, and is given voluntarily.

But doing the Amish protest thing in the Supreme Court is a lot of hard work, and you have to make the Court believe you. You have to actually live in the particular manner, and according to a sound philosophy, that compels you to protest peacefully. It helps to have talented lawyers on your side; often these are people who were raised Amish and left the community to join the "English," as they call us.

Discussion of the Amish and Medicare at first blush may seem far afield from the effect of taxes on your food budget, but remember that food producers have to pay into the government social-welfare system. That's another reason food provides a fertile resource for discussion of government's foibles—there's almost no government program that doesn't relate to your gustatory life, directly or indirectly. And that's why it's so easy for me to claim that our food supply would be half as expensive in a completely free market as it is in our economy today.

GOVERNMENT NANNYING

We've already seen government nannying at the industry level, in the form of compulsory subjection of producers to government safety inspections. I've also claimed (rather a safe claim, really) that allowing free markets to handle the inspections would result in a food supply that is less expensive, yet safer, than the one we have now. Government still has a nannying opportunity remaining—at the individual level, telling us what and how much we should eat. Can you imagine criminal penalties for overeating? Don't laugh at that prospect just yet—with the War on Drugs, we already have the government empowered to exact criminal penalties for smoking marijuana in our own homes.

Go ahead and think about a government War on Fat, similar to the War on Poverty and the War on Drugs, both of which worsened the problems they were supposed to solve. In Great Britain, where obesity isn't quite the problem it is in the US, the call has already gone out for government to save us from our appetites. Will Hutton, writing in 2002 for England's *The Guardian*, has called for his government to step in and put a stop to obesity. It's not enough for Hutton to recommend that warning labels be required on high-fat foods similar to the warning labels on cigarettes, and that fatty snacks be accorded special taxes. He seems almost to recommend medication for obesity, and it's unclear from his discussion whether he believes the medication should be entirely voluntary on the part of obese folks.

Hutton presents his opinion in complete seriousness. He doesn't grasp that he contradicts himself: He knows his eating and drinking habits aren't the best, but he blames it on "modernity" rather than on a lack of willpower. He can't be busier than American CEOs, but there are American CEOs who are not obese. Tony Blair, the British Prime Minister, is probably busier than Hutton as well. He's not obese. Neither are George W. Bush, Bill Gates, or a host of other people who live extremely busy lives yet have sedentary jobs—the same recipe Hutton blames for his own obesity. Those other busy and important people aren't fat, yet Hutton still deliberately places the blame squarely on: modern times. His solution—taxes, for example—won't actually stop him from getting fatter. The American poor, as I discuss later, are fatter than the American wealthy. Money won't make a difference.

I have difficulty discussing the topic with a straight face. It has already been recommended by the occasional American academician that we put higher taxes on fatty foods, but just imagine the complications, which I *can* discuss with a straight face. The clinically obese with behavioral problems will be disproportionately taxed, as some of them will continue to have difficulty mustering the willpower to avoid bad food. Thus, the tax amounts to a transfer of wealth from the identified victims to their "benefactors" in government. What of butter? There is no higher-fat food (100% of calories in butter come from fat, in case anyone didn't know this), but butter is a staple; as far as I know, it's still one of the foods available to food-stamp recipients because it's regarded as wholesome by government; and higher taxes and the consequent reduced consumption would be a shock to the dairy industry.

But we don't really need to explain the folly of government-enforced dietary regimes. The war on drugs is bad enough; how much more must we be reminded that the government owns our bodies? And given the successes of the wars on drugs and poverty—both wars having worsened the problems they were meant to solve[3]—we should expect the same success with any other social-engineering "wars" the government declares.

Let's consider some other issues. American political columnist George Will has a famous fear of genetic engineering of people, as he's written in his syndicated columns. He finds it horrific that parents might someday be able to ensure their children are intelligent, tall, or attractive (I wonder whether he would be opposed to parents being able to ensure their children aren't deformed, born with brain defects, etc.). If obesity is found to be predominantly a genetic issue, wouldn't Will Hutton want to use genetic engineering to wipe it out?

To satisfy both George Will, who doesn't want physical improvements in mankind, and Will Hutton, who does, we would have to let the obese eat all they want and kill themselves off early so as to select them out of the population. That would solve the obesity "problem" through eugenics without relying on politicians or scientists. Obviously, that whole idea is absurd; but it is the only sort of thing that could satisfy anyone who wants to achieve a species-wide human bio-

---

3.   See *www.Reason.com* for an excellent archive of material relating to the War on Drugs.

logical objective with the help of government, as both George Will and Will Hutton do.

Frankly, some people don't mind being obese, at least not too much. Given the complete inevitability of losing weight whenever you expend more calories than you take in (it's a law of physics, after all), those who are overweight are making choices on a daily basis. Occasionally fighting a spare tire myself, I understand the unpleasantness of those daily choices. It is natural that physical effort is aversive while eating and relaxing are enjoyable; otherwise, we could expect lions and tigers to chase after the strongest, fastest zebras in the herd, which of course they don't do.

And as our economies become more productive, there is more food available, there are more passive leisure activities to accompany eating, and more jobs require desk work rather than manual labor. All of these are good things; as just one example, work-related fatalities have been decreasing in the US for a century. And obese people are choosing for themselves to remain obese, when the answer—diet and exercise—is available to everyone for free (lest I get any emails about expensive diets: if you keep eating the same things you're eating now, it can only cost less to eat less of those things).

Rather than blame efficiency and instinct, and especially poor personal discipline, Hutton blames "modernity," which sounds like a euphemism for capitalism. His primary scapegoat is the long work week, which takes time that might otherwise be available for both exercise and healthy food preparation. The result is that each of us is pushed, involuntarily, toward high-fat convenience foods. Hutton places himself among the time- and ambition-starved and calorie-over-blessed. He claims it requires a "great effort of self-discipline" to overcome modernity's negative impact.

I'm forced to ask: Why do life expectancies for developed countries keep increasing in the face of obesity? The answer: medical advances. What makes medical advances possible? The answer: lots of people doing pure and applied research—scientists studying everything from the properties of a new petroleum-derived polymer to the behavior of isolated cells. What kind of economy provides the wherewithal that makes such opportunities possible? The answer: A free one. These questions and answers are so obvious that even George Will and Will Hutton ought to have considered them.

Life carries risk. The rumor is, we'll all die. Would we prefer the risk of the slow, predictable, and avoidable killer, obesity; or the risk of unseen diseases we can't predict or control? Asked another way, do Hutton and Will believe that the kind of government that could manage our diets and arbitrarily prohibit some kinds of genetic research while mandating other kinds still avoid the inevitable unexpected consequences of intervention and provide an economy that fosters only that research and technological advancement that Hutton and Will deem worthwhile? Finally, does Hutton believe any government really can or should force people to stop overeating, and does George Will believe any government can or should stop the progress of science?

I'll be direct: Calls for government nannying of individual dietary choices are idiotic, and guaranteed to do far more harm, both practical and moral, than good. The same goes for the government's preventing or controlling anything people are willing to pay money to enjoy. The same goes, but even more so, for attempts to prevent medical research that may save lives.

Some of the unintended consequences would be amusing if they weren't tragic: With high enough taxes on junk food, we'd see a black market for mayonnaise, and eventually we'd have nonviolent mayonnaise offenders as a huge percentage of the inmates in federal prisons, just as today we have nonviolent marijuana offenders as a huge percentage of inmates.

Protecting us from our own dietary choices—protecting us from ourselves—is only one angle government nannies are using to increase their power over our lives while decreasing our economic freedom with specific regard to food. Another angle: protecting us from each other! It's already in the minds of some movers and shakers. Various researchers have long reported that poor Americans are more likely to be fat than non-poor Americans.[4] You know what's next: To make it even more politically incorrect to say anything negative about fat people or poor people, we're now to be told that those of us who are not poor are responsible when a poor person gets fat.

First, some background: Greg Critser has written the book *Fat Land* (Houghton Mifflin, 2003), in which he blames obesity among the poor on the high calorie content of cheap fast food and the reluctance of homeowners to have their property taxes raised so government schools can afford, among other things, nutrition and exercise programs that might help poor children develop better eating and exercise habits. He also blames baby boomers for fostering a culture of overeating.

Fox News Network reported in January 2003 that Douglas Besharov, a researcher at University of Maryland, has also decided that poor fat people are the

---

4.   Just as one example, the *New England Journal of Medicine* seems to consider the inverse relationship between obesity and socioeconomic status in the US a given. See, for example, Obesity and Socioeconomic Status—A Complex Relation, September 30, 1993, pp. 1036–1037.

government's fault. Food stamp programs and free school breakfast and lunch programs encourage overeating, especially with the present lack of accompanying government-provided nutrition education, according to Besharov. Among his proposed solutions is to give the poor more cash and less food stamps.

There are some things Critser and Besharov need to get straight: Nobody in America forces food into any fat person's mouth. Every fat person has to make a decision, and exert an effort, to procure, chew, and swallow every bite he consumes. If the fat person is getting fat on McDonald's burgers, he is making the additional effort of driving to the restaurant and paying money for something nobody thinks is especially nutritious. Nobody is forcing any fat person to do any of that.

Of course, I jump eagerly onto the blame-the-government bandwagon. It was recently brought to my attention that the government's food pyramid results in the same carbohydrate-fat-protein calorie balance that scientists recommend for fattening pigs for slaughter. Of course the government is giving us bad information (the food pyramid is for everyone, not just the poor). And when you provide free anything, such as lunches and food stamps, you'll get takers.

Government handouts are a big problem for the poor (and not just the poor, since the rest of us are forced to foot the bill). Lotteries generally attract the poor, and some poor folks spend absurd amounts of money trying to win. This is partly ensured by the fact that some state governments advertise lotteries in get-rich-quick terms that are against the law for casinos to use in advertisements.

Government income tax allowances for dependents have already given rise to a black market in social security numbers: Hucksters pay poor, ignorant women a few bucks to learn the social security numbers of their children, and the hucksters then claim the children as dependents on their income taxes. The Earned Income Tax Credit—a wealth-redistributing welfare payment—has resulted in many people working for part of the year, then quitting work just before they earn enough to disqualify them for the credit. Bartenders in resort towns in Florida work through the tourist season, and collect unemployment during the off-season. And we've all seen people pay for groceries with food stamps, then drive away in a new car.

But back to the poor fat people: Most of them watch television copiously, and there are thousands of daily messages on television extolling diet and exercise (among the millions hawking get-thin-quick programs that don't always require much dieting or exercise). If you asked, and they didn't think they could get something out of it by lying, I'd expect that few poor people would know that the Atkins diet has been shown to reduce blood cholesterol, but I'd expect they all know that eating less and exercising more will result in weight loss and improved overall health.

I therefore, hereby, forthwith, verily, and vigorously refuse to take responsibility for any poor person's being fat, or even for their being poor. Poor Americans live far better than kings lived a scant 100 years ago. According to the government's own data, over 90% of Americans living below the government-determined poverty line own color televisions, and over 75% own VCRs.[5] If a poor person can read, he can get a college degree in this country, and the poorer he is, the less he'll have to pay for it (if he has to pay anything at all). He should take a nutrition course while he's there.

Trial lawyers and left-wing academics have created a victimization culture that encourages self-appointed critics to blame everyone but fat people for being fat. For their part, the lawyers and academics grew up being told that government is the solution to every problem a person encounters. I have a better solution: Look in a mirror. Make it a big mirror. And get all those fat people off our backs!

GOVERNMENT FOOD

A list of your favorite foods reveals things about your personality. If you eat a narrow variety of foods, you probably aren't very adventurous. Whether you can endure eating raw habanero peppers says more about your oral chemistry than about your personality, but whether you like foods to be as spicy as you can tolerate may say something about how vigorously you consume life. Such speculation is interesting enough, but it might be more interesting to speculate on what the food you offer to others says about you. Public schools offer food, so I checked some of their websites to see what their offerings had to say about them.

Maple Wood School in Somersworth, New Hampshire, has an online menu page. Their menu selections violate both nutritional and gustatory sensibilities: On one day, they served pepperoni pizza with coleslaw and ice cream. On another, macaroni and cheese and a peanut butter sandwich.

North Elementary School in Alamogordo, New Mexico, offered "corn stick pie" with green beans and fruited gelatin. Some of the other days' menus seemed nutritionally inoffensive, and they had a southwestern flair, but their administrators try to weasel politically-correct social indoctrination into the menu with such items as "potato smiles." Fruit Rainbows, Inclusive Salad, and Alternative Pie

---

5.   A summary is available from the National Center for Policy Analysis at
      http://www.ncpa.org/pi/welfare/!wel4.htm, accessed May 2004.

can't be far behind. Beware the hazards of indoctrination by foodstuffs. Egalitarian egg rolls, collective cake...

Remarkably, the food at Oswego High School in Oswego, New York, didn't look so bad—plenty of protein and good old fat, and lots of fruit. Their choices weren't perfect, as potato chips constitute the "bread" item one day each week. More interesting is what the menu revealed about the educational attainment of the people in charge: They offered "toss salad," as opposed to tossed salad; and "mash potatoes," instead of the mashed kind. Fortunately, the peaches are already "chilled," so you don't have to chill them yourself.

Were I to die and be sent to a public high school as punishment for my sins, I would wish to go to New Iberia Senior High in New Iberia, Louisiana. In a single week: On Monday, they served red beans and rice with sausage, muffins, and peaches; Tuesday, spaghetti with meatballs, green beans and potatoes, salad, garlic bread, and fresh oranges. Wednesday was baked pork chops, rice and gravy, black-eyed peas, carrot-raisin salad, and rolls. That's better than most of us eat. Then again, New Iberia is in the deep south, so it shouldn't be surprising to learn they do food better than schools in such places as New York and New Hampshire. (I explain in later chapters why Southern food is superior.)

Emporia High School, in Emporia, Kansas, is a tribute to the triumph of junk food over everything. In a single week, the "meat" items included corn dogs, pizza, and chicken-part nuggets, most likely deep fried.

Olmstead Falls Middle School in Olmstead Falls, Ohio, has decent lunches, but their breakfasts are a paean to the fear of protein. I was able to find eight days' worth of breakfast menus, and not a single one included meat, cheese, or eggs.

Montevideo Public Schools in Montevideo, Minnesota had on the online menu "raisen" bread and "crannberries"—they should turn to New Iberia for help with spelling. Lowville Academy and Central School, in Lowville, New York, went all out to avoid grammatical and typographical problems: The online menu page was blank.

Clarksville, Arkansas public schools list ingredients separately, perhaps to make the menu seem more comprehensive: On Friday at the middle school, they listed "hamburger, bun, lettuce, pickles, french fries, catsup, fruit, milk." On the same day, at the high school, the menu was "chicken sandwich, mayonnaise, french fries, catsup, lettuce, pickle, peaches, milk." And yes, they offered trailer food: "Frito chili pie/taco sauce, tossed salad/cheese, refried beans, pineapple, milk." Frito chili pie, by the way, is something you probably do not want to sample, but it is characteristically southern. Nor do you want to wash down pineapple with milk.

The prices at most of these cafeterias ranged from a high of $2 for regular children to a low of 30 cents for children with a government get-out-of-poverty-free card. Thus, be reminded that you're paying for these gustatory and digestive human rights violations the government calls lunches, regardless whether any of your own children are eating them.

Trust government with anything, and you'll be disappointed. Government schools pay good money to hire government-certified nutritionists. I would expect these nutritionists to have some understanding of nutrition and—dare we ask—decent menu combinations. And you'd think they could spell, at least the names of the food items. Don't trust private schools, either; I checked a few. Just feed the children at home, while you home school them.

THE ALTERNATIVE TO GOVERNMENT

This list of government intrusions is far from exhaustive, but by now you have the basic idea: Government wants to meddle in your culinary affairs. The government people doing the meddling, and writing all the new laws and recommendations, have a variety of motives. Surely some government employees, and people who founded certain government agencies, have had your best interests at heart. Unfortunately, we can never expect a few government employees to have better information than we do. We actually do the living they're trying to regulate. Other government employees, such as whoever paid plum farmers to burn thousands of acres of productive trees, may deceive themselves that they're doing some moral good, but no good can come of destroying food-producing capacity with the sole purpose being to spike the prices you and I have to pay.

Next, we go to the market, the only alternative to government. In standard economic terms, the market is you and me—people with jobs, doing our jobs as our employers and customers demand, then going out and being customers ourselves. Every buying and selling decision we make is based on the best information we have at hand, and we use that information in every decision we make. Some decisions we don't consider very carefully, such as which soft drink to purchase, while we devote extensive time to others, such as a car or home purchase. Government thinks it can help with these decisions, and often government makes the decisions for us.

Unbeknownst to government, we have more and better information than government does, and we make good decisions most of the time. Of course we do: Our own money, enjoyment, health, and safety are at stake. Further, there are

280 million of us. When we vote as a group for the VCR, automobile, and home style of our choice, our choices are awfully good: They represent the pooled wisdom of 280 million brains and 280 million wallets, and nearly every brain thinks the accompanying wallet is too small. We're nothing if not motivated.

And there's no better way to illustrate the power of the market—the power of all of us, thinking for ourselves, seeking solutions, and exploiting opportunities—than to look at the food itself.

3

The Brilliance of Markets: The Food Itself

Individual food items and recipes, and regional and national cuisines, represent the market—all the producers, sellers, and customers, you and me, all thinking and experimenting, all doing our best to make money, save money, make good meals, and have a good time. I discuss regional and national cuisines in later chapters. Here, I use individual food items and dishes to explore some interesting economic principles; highlight wonderful combinations and recipes; celebrate human ingenuity and good taste; and further illustrate the problems with government interventions into our gustatory lives.

FREEDOM CABBAGE!

To review: Food is a very big deal. Not only must we eat it often—and the more active of us must do so in sizeable quantities—but rarely do we fail to enjoy it, if we have any control at all over our choices. Food-related behavior can tell you a lot about people, from the individual level to the level of an entire nation. One foodstuff in particular, cabbage, tells interesting stories about people, freedom, culture, and history.

The round-headed cabbages we know are not a natural occurrence. Wild cabbage, which still grows along the shores of the Mediterranean, looks somewhat like celery, with big stalks and relatively few leaves. Endive or romaine lettuce, available at your local grocery, looks much like wild cabbage. The round-headed stuff wouldn't have evolved on its own, I'm sure. It's a ball of leaves, tightly wound on top of each other, the vast majority not contributing to the plant's nutrition through photosynthesis. Round-headed cabbage isn't even an evolutionary dead end; it's more of an evolutionary "what?" No, we humans selectively bred the wild stuff until we developed the round-headed stuff. We did so because we wanted to. This unnatural selection began more than 2,000 years ago.

A robust, free-thinking man would say that's exactly what vegetables are for. They're here for us, not for themselves. People rule, and that includes ruling cabbage, if it suits us. Cabbage is highly nutritious when eaten raw, and various national and regional cuisines have made culinary art from it, from Prussian sauerkraut to the ubiquitous American coleslaw (yes, I know, the Dutch may be at the bottom of that, "kool sla" and whatnot, but they don't make or eat it like we do, even though they put mayonnaise on french fries). Cabbage is a tribute to the victory of genetic engineering over vegetable nature, even if the engineering was done the slow, old-fashioned way, one cabbage generation at a time.

What's more, cabbage owes its status as a genetic oddity and culinary staple not to governments, monarchs, or consortia (discussed later). For hundreds of years in Europe, cabbage was seen as vulgar food, not suitable for polite people. Like potatoes, cabbage was for the unwashed peasants, and those uneducated peasants were the ones who accomplished both the genetic engineering and most of the culinary applications of it.

There are other lessons to be learned from cabbage. The Italians have made the best of it. They developed broccoli and cauliflower, and yes, those are cabbages. Broccoli and cauliflower for the chef and eater, as you know, are very different from the round-headed cabbages. Excellent raw or lightly steamed, broccoli and cauliflower don't cook, look, or taste like other cabbage varieties, and the nutrition is denser. You'd have to chew through a softball-sized wad of round cabbage (or an entire head or two of iceberg lettuce) to get nutrition equivalent to that in a few bites of broccoli or cauliflower.

The superior Italian cabbage developments didn't stop there, either—radicchio, that little purple-red lettuce, is bitter, peppery, and wonderful in a pungent salad. Try it with arugula (a dark-green, spicy leaf; the word comes from a Latin word for "cabbage") and goat cheese with a fig crust, as I had in a restaurant once; a vinaigrette dressing goes well with that. And at the other end of the culinary delight spectrum, I can only guess what Brussels sprouts say about Belgians. Those slimy, garbage-smelling little vegetable balls probably wish they were never developed. Perhaps these little gustatory abominations were developed at the request of inbred royalty.

Compare the development of cabbage in Europe (it has been developed all over the world, actually) with the political circumstances we now face in America. As we saw earlier, plum growers thought they'd sell more dried plums and dried plum juice if they could get rid of the name "prune." Our benevolent national government almost prevented this—tried to prevent food growers giving their own product its proper name. Can you imagine how deliberately and vigorously government would complicate your life if you tried to develop a new vegetable? (We get a clue from how difficult it is for companies like Monsanto to genetically engineer a new trait into an existing vegetable.)

Cabbage teaches valuable lessons about who we are, who we have been and should be, and where we're going. Lowly as it is, stinky and sometimes flavorless as it may seem to the 21st century palate, cabbage is an object lesson in its own right.

TEA

By now you can guess that the lessons to be learned from food are limitless. Almost any food you can name, if you study its history, has something to say about economics, politics, history, or culture. For whatever reason, tea, particularly the plain old regular types we all know (such as the "black" tea found in cheap boxes of 1,000 teabags at the local grocery megamart), seems to teach more lessons by its history than almost anything else we could eat or drink.

The first thing tea history demonstrates is that free trade and free markets are reliably and impressively resourceful. Tea first became known to a few in the west in the 1500s, and by 1620 it was exported from China to most all of Europe—on private ships. When entrepreneurs saw an opportunity, even in the face of months-long voyages, dangers, hardships, crude technology, and monstrous business risks (imagine coming back from a voyage and finding the product was out of fashion!, never mind the perpetual risk of piracy), the product found its market.

Another tea history lesson is that without government micromanagement of money and markets, things get less expensive; markets for goods and services approximate the perfect-competition model, and prices approach marginal cost.[1] In the first decades of the 1600s in Holland, tea was enjoyed by only a wealthy few, as it cost over $100 per pound. By the later decades of the same century, tea

---

1.   Marginal cost is the cost of making one more unit of a thing, or providing one more unit of service. For example, if you're a masseur, you have fixed costs of renting a boutique, buying equipment, etc. The actual cost of one more massage, though, is whatever that amount of time is worth to you right now. The marginal cost of making a 10,000th aluminum can today is mainly the cost of the aluminum that goes into the can.

was so affordable it was available in restaurants. Things keep getting more expensive for us today because the government keeps messing with our money—printing more of it at Greenspan's will to pay off debts—and absorbing half our productivity.

Tea keeps on teaching: There's nothing government can do that private enterprise can't do better. The John Company, in the 1700s, was granted by the government of Great Britain a monopoly on all trade to the Orient. Built mainly on the tea trade, the John Company was permitted—and able!—to occupy and govern territory, coin money, build forts, declare war, pass laws, and more. True, without government-sponsored monopoly power, a single firm wouldn't have been able to develop all those capacities as quickly or easily, but this is still more evidence that individuals and corporations can accomplish whatever needs doing, without government providing the infrastructure or funding.

And as with war history, tea history is written by the victors. The British East India Company, the one we've all heard about, was not the biggest player in the tea business during its entire history. In the early 1700s, the John Company was the big one, and East India, facing bankruptcy, was forced to appeal to the government for help. The companies were merged, and East India—the name of the combined company—was the biggest player by 1773 (and the same company that lost money as a result of the Boston Tea Party, after which coffee was declared America's favorite drink). Since East India won the right to keep its name, and because our revolutionary history was written by the victors in America, few Americans or Brits have ever heard of John Company.

But the tea history lessons continue, next reminding us that government corporate welfare hurts the consumer (that's you). The John Company and East India, after the government-brokered and -enforced merger, were granted monopoly rights over all trade with India and China. The result: The price of tea remained artificially high for Brits all over the world, including those in America fighting for their independence. It's worth keeping in mind that monopolies simply don't arise without the help of coercive government.

Tea's history in the US proves that a free economy makes your life better. It was America that invented iced tea and the paper teabag, the two most important innovations in tea history from the perspective of the average American Southerner. It is noteworthy that both these inventions surfaced before World War I, when the federal government began its twentieth-century booming expansion into internal economic and external political affairs.

Aside from powdered instant tea and new marketing of the same old products, there appear to have been virtually no additional substantial innovations in the

American tea industry until the 1980s and '90s, which brought us mass-market herbal "teas" (herbal teas aren't really tea), fruit-flavored teas, single-serving prepared iced tea bottles and cans, and more. Perhaps the governmental shocks to the economy of WWI, the Depression, WWII, and the welfare state of 1950 onward kept teamen on their heels for most of the century.

The history of tea reinforces even cultural lessons, such as that you can expect the South to make anything in its own special way. Along with mint juleps, pork barbeque, watermelon, and cooking with lard, the South made tea its own, in the form of sweetened iced tea. There's no restaurant in the South that won't assume you mean sweetened when you order iced tea, and there's no place you can go where iced tea isn't the most popular beverage.

Finally, tea reminds us that if you dig a little, the history of a single food item can teach more than a textbook, and the lessons strike you immediately and intuitively. If boring old tea can teach us this much in a few minutes, imagine what something nourishing, like beef, could say. (We'll get to beef later.)

BIRDS

I'm a red-meat guy. Why anyone would make a habit of cooking and eating a filthy, feathered, salmonella-ridden critter is a mystery to me. I refer to chickens and turkeys, of course; ducks are not salmonella-ridden, and they're beautiful and delicious.

Chicken and turkey must be fully cooked, to avoid risk of possibly deadly food poisoning (if you get poisoned by a bird, be prepared to lose 20 pounds of muscle and spend two weeks in the hospital). This means that chicken and turkey are usually going to be dry and tough if cooked at home, unless you've developed tremendous skill.

Aside from being generally unpleasant as animals; aside from being difficult to prepare well; aside from being fairly flat in flavor and texture; and aside from their tendency to contaminate your entire kitchen, chicken and turkey are great! Bodybuilders and dieters eat vast quantities of these creatures, because the white meat, dryly overcooked, is nearly 100% protein. Further, given its complete tastelessness, chicken white meat is superior to even turkey in its flexibility—it can be used in almost any recipe. And in terms of grams of complete protein per dollar, a whole chicken is a nutritional (if not gustatory) bargain.

Further, since whole chickens are inexpensive and easy to find, you can make plenty of use of the complete bird. First, bake it: Shove an entire stick of unsalted butter under the skin on top of the chicken. Put it on a rack inside a big baking dish. Pour some white wine into the dish, as much as you can but not enough to touch the bottom of the chicken. Cover the entire thing with foil. Bake at whatever temperature and for whatever duration you're supposed to bake a chicken of the size you have.

You can strain the juices in the bottom of the pan and reduce with a little flour to make a gravy. Take all the meat from the chicken, and simmer the bones in a large pot of water with a bottle of dry white wine, with perhaps a few whole peppercorns and a few sautéed onions and jalapenos. After a few hours, remove the bones, strain the liquid, and reduce until the liquid has some nice color and flavor. You now have chicken stock; use it for chicken soup, sauces, whatever.

When that chicken, baked in that fashion, comes out of the oven, it is as tender, juicy, and flavorful as a reptile can be. I've done it that way a couple of times, and it makes me forget all about beef (for 30 minutes, anyway). Reheat it the next day in the oven in a bowl, covered with gravy. It will be tender and delicious again.

What to do with any leftover meat? You can do anything with chicken. Dice yellow and red bell peppers, onion, jalapeno, smash up some garlic, and sauté everything in clarified[2] butter and olive oil. Serve over pasta with a marinara sauce. Sprinkle with fresh oregano and basil at presentation. (For an interesting enhancement, dice a nectarine and add it to the marinara early in the simmering.)

Aside from their culinary modesty, chicken and turkey manage to teach us object lessons of their own. What we have done in developing these animals for the mass production of food is to produce prey without the means to escape predators. They're so fat and meaty, the chickens can't fly, and some farmed turkeys get so hefty they can't even walk. Hunting them is akin to picking watermelons. They're inexpensive in terms of protein per dollar, they're easy to find in grocery stores, and if not as tasty as red meat, at least they're inoffensive.

Thus, mass-farmed chickens and turkeys are yet another example of mankind's mastery of the environment. For the sake of efficiency and profit, we've bred unprecedented animals, entirely useless to themselves and unable to survive on their own, but useful for those of us who care to eat them. These birds have

---

2.   To clarify butter, melt a stick of it (unsalted—the salted kind sometimes isn't as high-quality as the unsalted) at a low temperature, say 150 degrees Fahrenheit, in the oven in a transparent glass measuring cup. When it's fully melted, you'll see granules at the bottom, froth on top, and clear golden liquid—clarified butter—in between. That clear liquid is what you want; reach in there with a spoon to get it. It's smoky, silky, and takes a lot of heat without burning compared to whole butter.

become nothing more than high-volume, low-priced protein bags for human consumption, filthy and flavorless though they may be.

I'm not ready to say "hail chickens and turkeys," but hats should be off to the ranchers and entrepreneurs who have brought about such marvels as these walking family meals. Of course, people began this work long ago. Our government, with its red tape labyrinth of testing, approval, licensing, and patenting, provides a powerful disincentive to anyone who might want to develop any new animals today.

Imagine, though, with a truly free market in food and science…perhaps a cleaned, refrigerated, whole 10-lb. cow or deer in the meat section of your local grocery store, suitable for baking or grilling; or a 90-lb. salmon, for roasting on a spit at a family reunion—the possibilities are endless and mouthwatering. It's too bad they're not as possible nowadays.

HOT COFFEE

As with so many other foods, such as tea, coffee offers examples of free markets and free minds at work, of people making life better for everyone at no one else's expense. Coffee is the most popular beverage in the world and has been around longer, and teaches more lessons, than you might expect. A brief reading of its history might even serve to reeducate our political leaders in the benefits of freedom and the folly of centralized anything.

The most popular legend for the discovery of coffee dates from c. 800 A.D. It is said that an Ethiopian (some accounts read Yemeni) goatherd noticed his goats frolicking merrily after eating some berries from a bush. He ate a few of the same berries, and found himself energized. This account shows up in every history of coffee, but is probably apocryphal: Archaeologists have established that Ethiopians were eating coffee berries thousands of years ago.

For centuries, Africans ate the beans raw. Commonly, they ground green coffee beans, mixed them with animal fat, and rolled them into small balls to eat as needed for energy, such as while traveling. That would have been the first-ever trail mix. Coffee was cultivated on, and traded from, the Arabian peninsula perhaps as early as 800 A.D., and it appears the Turks were the first to use it widely to make beverages, sometimes adding spices. The first coffee shop opened in Constantinople around 1475.

One of the lessons to be learned from coffee is the ineffectiveness of outlawing victimless vices (it is a bit of a stretch to consider coffee a vice; it's a pretty benign addiction). The Ottoman Sultan tried to outlaw coffee in Turkey in 1543, and by 1554 the coffee business was booming there. Supply and demand exploded, perhaps because the ban could only have made business immensely more profitable.

Remember the War on Drugs? Because of the risk premium tied to cocaine distribution, cocaine commands an extremely high price on the street, and we get only the purest stuff (as long as you're going to risk imprisonment for smuggling a briefcase full of something, you'll prefer to take that risk for something worth $5,000,000 over something worth $50). The Scots occasionally tried to ban golf, too, but we now consider Scotland the birthplace of golf as an organized sport, even though evidence shows it might have originated as a pastime in Denmark.

The spread of coffee around the world over the next 200 years is a testament to the resourcefulness and persistence of entrepreneurs. By 1750, coffee had reached most of the places in the Americas where it is cultivated today. There were brief earlier experiments in lowlands in Brazil where coffee grew poorly, but by the time it was known that high altitudes worked better, it was a profitable business for everyone cultivating it in the Americas. By 1750, coffee was being sold across Europe, and was being cultivated in India and Java. The first trader to take it to India had to smuggle it out of Arabia, marking another case of a government's restrictions failing to work as intended. Even taxes have been implicated, as when coffee was declared America's national beverage in 1773, in conjunction with the Boston Tea Party.

Entrepreneurial achievements are scattered throughout coffee's history, and are not limited to smuggling and shipping. In Vienna in 1675, before coffee was well known there, one Franz Georg Kolschitzky helped the Viennese fend off a Turkish siege. In their haste, the Turks left behind bags of dried ground coffee. Kolschitzky, having lived in Turkey, knew what the bags contained, and when asked to name his reward for helping save the city, he asked for the coffee. The Viennese probably thought Franz was daft. He opened a coffee house and was quite successful.

Coffee has come a long way. Further developments since the days of eating raw beans include roasting and grinding (from as early as A.D. 500); adding spices (1400s); filtering (1600s); vacuum-packing in tin cans (1900); and instant coffee (1901). The percolator dominated American home coffee making from when it was first electrified in about 1908 until the drip coffee maker took over.

The drip machine was invented just after WWII, but it wasn't until the early 1970s that it was developed to the point that it was viable on the market. Since canning and processing tend to reduce quality, over the last couple of decades the luxury trend has been toward local roasting (Starbucks opened in 1971) and grinding your own beans at home. In 1900, it was a luxury to prepare it at home without going to all that trouble; today, people who can taste the difference believe it's worth doing it the old-fashioned, less-convenient way.

The history of coffee is more peaceful than the history of many other commodities, such as oil, iron, gold, and Irish potatoes. Still, government had a part in the spread of coffee, usually through futile attempts to outlaw it. The history of tea may have been a little more on the violent side also, again because of government involvement. But for both coffee and tea, you can be assured that private individuals and corporations are responsible for the fact that you can enjoy either one affordably, conveniently, in abundance, in variety, and at a high quality, anytime, anywhere.

COFFEE MADNESS

Coffee remains the best selling beverage in the world. Once you get past the bitterness (which is usually imparted by too-high temperatures applied to the beans during brewing), as most of us manage to do in our teen years, good coffee provides unmatched flavor and aroma, comfort, and familiarity, along with an energizing caffeine boost without which many of us would struggle mightily to overcome morning and after-lunch drowsiness. This benign addiction inspires the best and the worst in mankind.

Both the best and the worst of men's tendencies are illustrated by poopoo coffee, as I call it, or Kopi Luwak (civet coffee), as it's called in Indonesia. The civet is a mammal, apparently a variety of cat that resembles a cross between an opossum and a rhesus monkey. Where there are both civets and coffee, civets eat big red coffee berries. Civets can't digest the beans, so the beans can be found on the ground after the civets have passed them through their digestive tracts.

According to reports, the beans are unaffected by the adventure, and are prized for the special flavor and aroma they impart when roasted, ground, and brewed. Such beans are probably the rarest of coffee varieties, and sell over the Internet for $300 per pound. It might as well be noted that if passing through the bowels of a cat didn't affect the flavor of the final product, these particular beans would be no more prized than other Indonesian coffees. People are paying high prices precisely because the beans have been so passed. (An aside: Perfume makers often add a tiny amount of an extract which, by itself, has a strong fecal aroma. Yep.)

This represents the worst of humanity, in my opinion, with regard to gullibility: People are paying $300/lb for, and consuming, things picked from animal crap. Such people might be expected to purchase expensive programs detailing the buying and selling of real estate with no money down, based on the unbiased and objective reporting of a late-night infomercial.

The best of humanity—the razor keenness of entrepreneurship and frictionless efficiency of free markets—is shown by the result that you and I, using the Internet and a credit card, can sit in our homes and procure these animal droppings with the click of a mouse. Where there's a demand, with or without government intervention, there will arise a supply. By the way, all the best jokes you may have thought up by now ("good to the last dropping," "crappuccino," "mountain thrown") have been used somewhere already.

Another coffee behavior exemplifying both the best and the worst of mankind was played out in Berkeley, California, in the Berkeley Initiative of 2002, as it might infamously be known someday. An unemployed Berkeley law-school graduate introduced a ballot initiative, voted on in November of 2002, that would have provided fines and imprisonment for restaurateurs who brew and sell coffee that is not either fair-trade priced, organically grown, or grown under a shade canopy that benefits wildlife. Fair-trade means the farmer(s) producing the coffee have been paid a "fair" price for it.

All of this means it can be guaranteed that had the initiative passed, customers would have been forced to pay more for coffee in Berkeley than anywhere else in the country. It also would have meant that inefficient local producers could stay in business long after a free market would have abolished them; they would then benefit at everyone else's expense. Fortunately, the initiative was soundly rejected by voters, though some local shops have signs in the windows saying "only 'fair' coffee sold here." That means it'll be more expensive than, even if it's not as good as, the stuff sold in the shop across the street.

This exemplifies the best in humanity in that there is no higher calling than selfless dedication to others. John 15:13: "Greater love hath no man than this, that he lay down his life for his friends." It might be said that every social program a leftist ever proposed exhibits on its surface a desire to do good for someone else who may be disadvantaged. It can also be said that every government social program ever proposed has as its fatal flaws that a moral injustice is perpetrated whenever an innocent person has his earnings confiscated by force for someone else's benefit; and that every social program that attempts to oppose market forces will introduce inefficiency into the market and have unintended consequences.

The failings underlying the Berkeley Initiative included arrogance, self-righteousness, ignorance of market functioning, and ignorance of history. You can bet that passage of this initiative would have hurt Berkeley merchants; helped Berkeley-area gas stations, as customers would have traveled more for cheaper coffee; hurt Berkeley sales tax revenues; helped coffee merchants in surrounding localities not affected by the initiative; increased traffic congestion and accidents as city dwellers left city limits to buy coffee; and increased the load on the court and penal systems as smugglers arose. The sizes of these effects always depend on the sizes of the costs added to legislatively disfavored producers—the higher the costs, the greater the effects. And what of the cost to civil liberties once Berkeley instituted a War on Unauthorized Coffee?

Wherever you are, be thankful if it's not Berkeley, and be thankful you are not sophisticated enough to pay $300/lb. for coffee passed through a jungle animal's bowels. Do what I do: Drink the free stuff at work, and occasionally splurge and pay 79 cents for the gourmet stuff at that convenience store on the way to work. Keep coffee number 1, and stay away from California and from coffee made from number 2.

PORK TARTAR

No, don't try to prepare raw pork at home. Yes, believe it when times change, and when markets are responsible for it. The story of pork safety is worth considering as an exemplar of human technological development, provided by individuals wanting to earn dollars from customers who offer them voluntarily.

In Old Testament times, as in much of the third world today, "kosher" was functionally synonymous with "safe." Whether it stems from a literal command from God, or from the results of generations of trial and error and observation, foods not considered kosher are indeed different. They have been shown in the lab to carry special health risks due to known, dangerous microbes. Pigs have always been a special case for me. After all, Southerners use pork fat to flavor all kinds of things, and pork barbeque has been a Southern delicacy for longer than anyone knows.

Progress marches on. People are eating raw oysters all around the Gulf coast, and have been for years. The market knows when water conditions mean the oysters aren't safe to eat. All manner of seafood-without-scales (i.e., non-kosher seafood) is eaten by the ton in America daily, and almost no one's ever met anyone who was sickened by a lobster since Walter Hagen won his first US Open after being so sickened 85 years ago. Duck is served medium-rare in restaurants, and I've eaten a seared, peppered venison filet that was fully raw on the inside.

Which brings us to pork, the one thing we've always been admonished never to undercook. Being cooked to well done, it has always needed to swim in fat while cooking to prevent its being dry as chalk. But for some years now, scientists and dieticians and butchers and restaurateurs have been telling us that pork doesn't need to be totally cooked; the internal temperature has only to get above a certain point, and it's fine without being well done.

So, I ordered a pork tenderloin dish at a local upscale, trendy restaurant, and I deliberately didn't specify degree of doneness. It arrived cooked to a perfect medium, I enjoyed every bite, and I suffered no ill effects; just as I didn't with the medium-rare duck and the raw venison.

Unless you're an experienced cook, and you have the right tools, you don't want to experiment at home with undercooked pork or any kind of completely raw meat. Unless you can compete with the professionals, let them do the work. You just enjoy it. When you do partake, keep the following in mind: The advances in sanitation—feeding, killing, cleaning, refrigeration, storage, transportation, preparation—that have made it possible to enjoy good foods, deliciously cooked, owe to the ingenuity and motivation of individual entrepreneurs in areas of research ranging from coolants to pressure gauges.

And definitely don't try raw pork at home. But here as in many places, the Italians (discussed in their own chapter later) beat everybody to the punch with their hams and sausages. You've eaten raw pork from Italy. When Italians produce hams ("prosciutto"), they salt raw pig legs and hang them up in a large building facing the sea with all the windows open. The hams hang there for two years. Gourmet restaurants sometimes refer to them as "air cured." When the Italians make some of their lunchmeats and sausages, they grind raw pork and pork fat with salt, pepper, and spices. Then they age it. Buy some salami, and enjoy. Don't even ask about bologna—that cliché you heard about sausages and laws being the things you don't want to see being produced is true.

The lesson? People make life better. Freer people make life better faster. And as the Italians keep demonstrating, advancing technology isn't the answer, it's the result. People—entrepreneurs, inventors, experimenters, and especially customers—are at the bottom of it all. Leave them alone to do their work, and watch your quality of life improve.

KILLER TOMATOES

The tomato, as we saw earlier in the Nix vs. Hedden case, teaches lessons about politics and economics. The lessons range broadly, from highlighting the temptation government largesse provides to businessmen hungry for competition-squashing leverage, to the willingness of bureaucrats to ingratiate themselves—at the direct economic expense of the public at large—to politically powerful voting blocs. There are other lessons the humble tomato teaches, lessons it would be remiss for any self-respecting politically incorrect gourmet to ignore.

The first lesson was taught by the history of tea: Entrepreneurs find markets for good products. In the days of months-long sea voyages, pirates, no control of disease, and slow and unreliable communications, the tomato was brought to Europe and gradually found its way into every continental cuisine. The process was slow, with the tomato taking 150 years from its first arrival on the continent (ca. 1550) to become a well-known item in every cuisine, but we must view this slow pace partly in light of the fact that the tomato is related to other poisonous plants, and was long rumored to be poisonous itself. Hence, its slow assimilation into European cuisine was due in part to conscious resistance by Europeans.

History lessons continue: How many of us knew that the tomato wasn't always a staple of Italian cuisine, but most likely originated in Peru? That the name, "tomato," seems to have originated with aboriginal South Americans? That the name "love apple," or "pomme d'amour," probably developed erroneously from the Spanish "pome dei Moro," or "apple of the Moors"? It was "pome d'oro" for many Europeans, suggesting that the golden, or yellow, tomatoes were the first ones to arrive. The first accounts have them eaten in Italy with oil, salt, and pepper. Of course, it was the Italians who elevated the tomato to its status in fine cuisine. This should be no surprise, as the Italians have elevated food preparation in general beyond levels seen in any other cuisine in the world.

And the tomato itself teaches us that God exists and that he wants us to be happy (as Benjamin Franklin said about beer). One of the best classical salads ever is as simple as it is delicious: sliced fresh tomatoes, sliced fresh mozzarella, fresh basil leaves, extra virgin olive oil, balsamic vinegar, salt, and pepper. But it's in marinara sauces that tomato cooking reaches perhaps its highest form. Here's mine:

Sauté, in clarified butter and olive oil, finely diced white or yellow onion and finely julienned and diced carrot (1/2 of a carrot-sized carrot to one medium onion). After a little glaze is achieved in the bottom of the pan, add a tablespoon or so of tomato paste (let it develop some color) and a smashed and diced clove or three of garlic. Put the garlic in at this stage, instead of at the beginning, and don't let it scorch; it can get bitter when browned. Deglaze with the wine of your choice, and a commercial vegetable stock; season with black pepper—salt shouldn't be necessary with the wine and stock. Add plenty of peeled/seeded/diced[3] roma tomatoes, and half a peeled and diced nectarine if you like a little sweetness in your marinara. Let simmer for an hour or longer; use a lid on the pot judiciously to get the degree of reduction and thickness you're after. When serving, garnish liberally with fresh basil and oregano.

For a variation on the same old marinara-over-pasta theme, try serving the marinara over a nice New York strip steak, 1-1/2 inches thick and grilled medium rare. For pasta prior to that steak marinara, try a fettuccini Alfredo[4] with two garnishes: marinated white grapes[5] on one side, and sliced black olives on the other. For a salad, try a few mixed bitter field greens and some radicchio with balsamic vinegar, extra-virgin olive oil, and black pepper.

Try an Italian salsa: Diced, seeded, and peeled roma tomatoes; diced red onion, garlic, and jalapenos; fresh oregano; white wine or white wine vinegar; and a little salt and pepper. Let marinate for at least a few hours.

The tomato may not be quite the exemplar of freedom that cabbage is, nor the distinctive cultural statement that pork barbeque and iced tea are, but it does have lessons to teach. Even without the object lessons, the tomato would remain well worth exploring in its own right as an affordable, flexible delicacy. Don't forget that it comes in several varieties, each with a recipe file of its own.

SHARK ATTACK

As everyone probably knows by now, shark attacks along our lovely gulf coast are becoming more frequent and deadly with each passing year. If you fly along the gulf coast in a helicopter, you can see sharks swimming around a few hundred

---

3. Cut the core end out of the tomato and drop it in boiling water until the skin just cracks; remove to cold water until it cools enough to be handled. Massage the tomato, core end down, over a trash can, and in a few seconds it will be peeled and seeded. Be careful not to drop the whole tomato into the trash can.

4. My Alfredo sauce omits the king of cheeses. Try it with butter, white wine, heavy cream, and a little salt and pepper.

5. Slice white grapes in half (this work goes faster than you expect) and marinate a few hours to overnight in white wine vinegar and black pepper. Drain before presentation.

yards out from the people swimming at the beach. It appears we should expect the attacks to become more common as time goes by. To make matters worse, it seems it's only a matter of a few elections before the mentally deficient PETA (People for the Ethical Treatment of Animals) types find a way to get the sharks protected, even if the sharks are never declared "threatened" or "endangered." Environmentalists have already expressed their sympathies with sharks.[6]

When you have an intelligent enemy, you should reason with him. Persuade him. Be more intelligent than he is, and you win without anybody getting hurt. If you're intelligent enough, you might be able to make him leave the contest thinking he won. On the other hand, when you have an indescribably stupid enemy who will never understand and never stop attacking you, you can only drive him away or kill him. There are no other options. Dolphins understand this about sharks. A dolphin will beat a shark to death by ramming the shark with his nose until the shark is dead—any shark, anytime, no immediately obvious purpose required.

I can't go attacking sharks myself. I'm not a diver, I'm not very near the coast, and I don't have the money for a .50-caliber sniper rifle and helicopter rental. However, I can do my part in making the sharks in the gulf a little less numerous, and here it is:

Shark Chili

Sauté, in clarified butter and olive oil:

- diced white onion
- diced fresh jalapeños
- diced green bell pepper
- freshly cracked black pepper

Deglaze with dry white wine, vegetable stock, and the juice of no more than one fresh lime; use plenty of liquid so you have something to reduce to intensify flavors. Sample the sauce to determine whether you need to add any sweetness to counter the lime's tartness.

Add fresh shark filets, and canned (drained and rinsed) white beans. Simmer uncovered (to reduce) until the filets are cooked through; longer if you have time, to be sure they're nice and tender. If you want a thick texture, mash some of the beans in the pot with a fork. Stir, and whatnot.

---

6.   See their views for yourself at http://www.peta.org/.

At presentation, throw on top some fresh cilantro and/or Italian parsley, and maybe some zest from the lime for extra color and flavor. Accompany with rice, cooked in the same wine and vegetable stock, but not the lime juice; garnish the rice with lime zest and shredded Romano cheese.

A good substitute for the rice would be Mexican corn, or better, a corn relish (e.g., mix a package of frozen yellow corn with a jar of a good picante sauce—good food doesn't have to be difficult to prepare). If you still need a vegetable, steam some fresh broccoli or cook up some fresh asparagus. Brussels sprouts would work, if you are in the superminority who can endure their slimy texture and dumpster aroma.

You don't even have to use my recipe. For those of you who haven't tried it, shark filets come across the teeth and palate like extra-tender, bleached-white beef, with a mild flavor. For those who don't care for fish, especially when badly prepared, you can be reassured that shark isn't fishy-tasting, and it doesn't get ruined easily. Any citrus-flavored chicken recipe you already enjoy should be even better with shark.

Perhaps by stimulating demand for shark meat, I can save some human lives at the beach. At the very least, I know the attempt would be enjoyable for adventurous home chefs, which is a worthwhile end in itself. You also get to enjoy making a pastime of thumbing your economic nose at the animal-first kooks. Political incorrectness is its own reward.

EAT MORE CHILI

Chili—the Tex-Mex olio that serves as cheap sustenance for some, comfort food for others, and an athletic challenge for a few nut cases among whom I count myself—manages to teach object lessons, directly and indirectly, about politics, economics, and culture, as does just about every food we've seen and will see. That being the case, chili is interesting to discuss in its own right, and topics related to it can be limitless if you free-associate a bit.

Aboriginal Central American cuisine, at least for royalty, was varied and probably delicious. Yucatan aborigines had among their favorites such delicacies as snapper cooked with oranges and cilantro, and an unsweetened hot beverage made from chocolate and hot peppers. The more arid areas that are now south Texas and northern Mexico offered a bit less variety, so we see lots of meat and beans. Hot peppers, tomatoes, onions, and some other fresh produce managed to make it to the area also.

The settlers from Europe who made it into the south Texas area are largely of German and Scot-Irish descent. It is interesting in this context that English, Irish, and German cuisines are large-scale gustatory crimes. People of these nationalities ridicule their own national foods, among which can be found haggis (potatoes, grains, and animal parts you and I would throw away, all cooked in a sheep's stomach) and various soggy, nonnutritive things among which we see, for example, dumplings. In all three places, cabbage, potatoes, and often unmentionable meats make up a great majority of the calories consumed.

By contrast, even the redneckiest Texan today—often a direct descendant of the gustatorially-differently-abled German and Scot-Irish immigrants—has his own complex chili recipe, and he can offer you numerous variations of it. Most variations on a given recipe involve meat preparation and the amount of pepper heat applied. There are contests all over Texas, some of which are won and lost over the amount of pepper heat, though judging almost always is more sophisticated than to be based solely on any one factor.

As a thing to do with beans and meat, chili is heroic. The basic flavoring mix we all recognize requires cumin, garlic, and some kind of hot pepper. Most commercial chili powders, without which you can do nicely if you use fresh ingredients, have these three items in them. Beef is generally required, but venison chili is found all over the southeast. Tomatoes and oregano, while nice, are not necessary ingredients. If you include cumin, garlic, and tomatoes, most people outside Texas will perceive your dish as chili; inside Texas, some recipes have only the two "classically" required ingredients: beef and peppers.

For tomatoes, people use fresh or canned; tomato sauce and tomato paste show up in many recipes. In the southeast, bell peppers are a common ingredient. I use fresh garlic, and sometimes cumin seed rather than ground cumin. For hot pepper, I use fresh jalapenos, though there are other peppers used, both fresh and powdered. Some people use bottled hot sauces, which I don't recommend because they impart a vinegar flavor of their own that isn't always consonant with everything else in the mix.

Most cooks include onions. Ground meat is common, though diced beef, especially filet mignon, is always nice. One of my favorite tricks is to use entire filet steaks, carefully trimmed. I simmer them for a few hours in beef stock, until they fall apart completely. Then I can begin putting together the actual chili. When liquid is needed, beef stock is common. I use red wine also. And some folks have other little tricks to add depth of flavor. For me, it's plenty of fat, from clarified butter and olive oil. Instant coffee and unsweetened cocoa have made appearances in many recipes. Oh, and some folks add salt and black pepper. Enough wine and/or reduced beef stock, though, and you don't need salt.

This brings us to beans, a matter of contention among chili aficionados. Some use them, some don't. Kidney beans are the most common, followed by pinto beans. You can use them from a can; I drain and rinse them first (on the rare occasions when I use them at all). Finally, I heat beans separately at the last minute, and add them just at presentation so they retain their texture.

Where chili came from is not well known. The earliest references to it mention only diced meat and hot peppers, from Texas in the 1820s or so; likely aboriginal. Recipes evolved as cowboys and settlers fiddled with ingredients. Entrepreneurs developed chili powders in the early 20th century, and the popularity of the dish has increased steadily ever since.

Chili is yet another example of the glories us common folk can generate when left alone for long enough. It's also an example of what can arise through the exchange of ideas and cultures. China was a world leader in technology, then closed its borders to trade 500 years ago. They have been backward on the world scene ever since, and have begun a recovery only in the last couple of decades. Free-market reforms get the credit.

Europe outstripped Africa through the past 3,000 years, partly because Europe's coastlines and inland waterways enabled trade, which carried with it the intermixing of cultures and ideas. Note that the center of ancient civilization in Africa—Egypt—arose along a waterway near an ocean, as did ancient Babylon.

Free trade in products, services, and *ideas* is what moves us forward, and nothing demonstrates that better than chili. There are wider variations on the theme, such as my own walnut chili (discussed next) and the shark chili discussed earlier. If you haven't developed a recipe of your own, the best way is to read dozens of recipes carefully, then go to the kitchen and make up your own. You can find chili recipe books on the web and in any giant bookstore, and you can find tons of recipes for free at foodtv.com. The real trick is to do it many times, experimenting with ingredients. If you're not an expert already, you can become one in a short time.

WALNUT CHILI

I am fully persuaded that of all national cuisines, Italian is the best the world has to offer. But this is true only when the basis of comparison is a known regional or national tradition—Chinese, Tex-Mex, French, or Southeastern American, for example. Italian is the best for several reasons, among them variety, preparation techniques, the ingredients themselves, the combinations of ingredients, and the way the Italians love cooking and eating.

Many Americans labor under the misnotion that French food is the finest cuisine, but that is the result of successful marketing (if effete snobbery qualifies as marketing). The French love to talk about, look at, and sell food. The Italians love to cook and eat it. For my money, anyone who will age pork and cheese for two years, and vinegar for twenty, is a food lover who merits emulation.

There is more to great food than recognizable regional traditions, however. Chefs around the world, especially in the less-tradition-bound US, are combining the best ingredients and techniques from everywhere and developing new dishes of their own. Combinations such as nuts and fish, meat and fruit, and others are appearing and providing surprising and delightful new tastes. Items such as Mexican salsa with hot peppers and a fruit base (peach or pineapple), and frozen barbequed chicken pizza, are on the shelves at your local Wal-Mart. Efficient international trade contributes to this trend, and some combinations that seem new really aren't. But many, probably most (I doubt anybody's counted), of the newest ideas are coming from the US.

I hate to use vulgar platitudes such as "thinking outside the box," but that is what's happening among chefs and entrepreneurs. And as anyone outside Washington, DC or a university knows, free thinking is best fostered by free markets in information and food. Even given our rapidly decreasing liberties in general, and mountains of government intervention in the food business, the US is still the best place to cook and eat.

Best of all, you don't need exotic ingredients, complicated cooking techniques, or expensive equipment to create gourmet cuisine. Unusual and delicious combinations can be created in your kitchen right now, unless you're a bachelor (my fridge has only expired food in it right now) or a vegetarian.[7] Basic ingredients and methods can surprise you. Here's my favorite original dish:

Walnut Chili

We've already seen that chili does not necessarily contain anything but meat and peppers, so I have no problem calling this "chili." Sear beef tenderloin filets in clarified butter and extra-virgin olive oil, in a great big porcelain (or other nonreactive) pot. When at least one side of each filet is nicely browned, cover with beef

---

7.   The book of Leviticus commands us to eat meat. End of discussion.

stock (not broth; stock is made from bones, and contains gelatin, so when it reduces, it thickens) and some dry Italian red wine.

Depending on how much you like black pepper, you can add some whole black peppercorns at this point. Black pepper is the nutritional equivalent of wood, as I seem to remember, so it should always be considered optional. Since it releases its flavor slowly, it's good to add it early. Using the peppercorns whole means you can get the flavor, and strain out the peppercorns later. Simmer all this for a few hours until the meat falls completely apart—you want this. You may need to add liquid occasionally, though keeping the lid on adds a little pressure inside the pot, which means the meat breaks down faster.

Sauté diced onion, jalapeno, broken walnuts, and fresh thyme in clarified butter and olive oil. Deglaze with some of the wine. Add all that to the beef.

Add diced fresh apple. The variety is up to you, but Gala and Cameo work well. Red Delicious is perfectly acceptable. Whether to peel the apples is also a matter of preference.

Simmer until the apples reach the texture you want; add liquid as desired. You can make it soupy, and the broth will be terrific. Thicken with a cornstarch slurry and/or whole butter if desired. I tend to prefer avoiding cornstarch. The butter and a real beef stock will make the liquid plenty viscous.

It's fun just to stir and smell what you have in the pot now. The beef will be so juicy, you won't need one of the dark, hopsy beers that go so well with this dish, but have one anyway. The juice will be dripping down your chin. It's great over the next few days, too. Garnish for presentation with a little more fresh thyme.

I can think of no good nutritional reason to eat a ton of bread, but a nice complement would be black bread with extra-sharp cheddar cheese melted on it, and some fresh black pepper cracked on top. For dessert, anything with homemade vanilla bean ice cream on the side would go well.

All you need is some creativity, common ingredients of good quality, and an Italianate love of cooking and eating to produce some of the world's best food. And even though I think my walnut chili is excellent using only a few ingredients available everywhere, there can be no doubt that increasing political and economic freedom will only increase the joy you can create in your kitchen with new combinations of ingredients.

Try my chili; see what you think. Try it as described[8] first, then try your own variations. And try some other new combinations of mundane ingredients. You can be a gourmet without shopping far and wide for exotic ingredients.

LIVERWURST

And as though it were some kind of exotic ingredient itself, there is surprisingly little information available about the history of liverwurst. Since it is a type of sausage, there is at least vicarious history on the Internet: Meat products and parts and other animal whatnottery (including organs and other things), ground into a paste with plenty of solid fat and hopefully some strong spices, have been stuffed into cleaned animal intestines and served as food probably for nearly as long as we've been cooking with fire.

Ah, but the eating: Salami and mortadella from Italy, which amount to raw pork (don't make it at home); patty-style breakfast sausage; "Italian" sausage with the hot pepper flakes in it (spectacular with sautéed bell pepper, onion, and garlic); summer sausage with cheese and barbecue sauce; and the poor man's pâté, Liverwurst. Liverwurst is different from the others in that it's spreadable (at least the good stuff is), and there's liver—among other things—in it.

The nutritional balance is another thing you don't want to know about, but true to my form, I'll proceed anyway: Around 75% of the calories come from fat. There's a ton of vitamin A in it, but it's the toxic kind. Carrots have a substance, beta carotene, that makes your body produce its own vitamin A. You don't need to worry about OD'ing on beta carotene. You don't really need to worry about OD'ing on vitamin A from liverwurst either, but it is at least possible to OD on vitamin A. Just so you know.

But, like cheesecake, the flavor and texture of liverwurst are worth its impeachable nutritional profile. Be careful what you buy: There are some imported German brands—go figure; Germans invented liverwurst—that are tough, slimy, and armpit-flavored. Good old Oscar Mayer is about as good as any you can find, when you can find it. (The Oscar Mayer liverwurst is referred to on the package as Braunschweiger, which a food encyclopedia will tell you is a subset of liverwurst, being always spreadable and supposedly reinforced with milk and eggs. You don't generally find milk and eggs in modern packaged liverwurst; but no matter.) The Oscar Mayer is a tad strong-flavored, as liverwurst must be, and

---

8.   I almost never give quantities of ingredients in recipes. How much you want is about the right amount.

goes well with hearty rye bread, raw white onions, and mustard. I take good old French's yellow mustard on my liverwurst. And beer.

At least one restaurant, my favorite Irish pub in Destin, Florida, serves it exactly that way: Liverwurst, raw onion, rye bread, and mustard. Their liverwurst sandwich deal includes a free beer. They pile a pound of meat on the sandwich (about 1520 calories), and to eat that entire pâté mound would probably initiate one of those near-death experiences you read about. But if you eat three of them, you get a free t-shirt and an Alka-Seltzer. They serve it with low cholesterol potato chips, so it's okay. I can get through about half the sandwich, usually after asking for extra bread. And beer. Then I return to the condo, lie on the couch, and have a two-hour near-consciousness experience.

Liverwurst—along with Beethoven's late string quartets, Michelangelo's art-works, and automated travel—is one of the greatest achievements in the panoply of "dead European male" culture:

At the dawn of the Age of Liverwurst, somewhere in north-central Europe, there were round-bellied, middle-aged, extremely European males enduring rela-tively harsh winters wearing garments that didn't cover their legs, gathered around a carcass. They set to work on all its inside parts and outside parts. Such men had a flair for making dead animal parts appetizing and giving them long shelf lives. (Some Italian dried sausages keep for many months at room tempera-ture; and remember prosciutto, mentioned earlier. As usual, Italians remain the most accomplished dead European males with regard to food, the glory of liver-wurst notwithstanding.)

It wasn't European males who invented beer, but it took Europeans to elevate it to the passion it is today. You can't swing a sausage in Belgium or Holland without knocking over a microbrewery, and each brewery custom orders special snifters for its beer(s) to highlight whatever character the brewer wants you to detect—different shapes accentuate particular aroma components differently, or so I hear. And as someone once said about a golf course without wind: Liverwurst without beer is like a face without a nose.

You can buy Alka-Seltzer anywhere.

Make yourself part of the great onward march of culture; relive the grandeur of ages past; feel a connectedness with the best of the untold generations before you, and those to come: Experience the glory of liverwurst, one of the greatest achievements ever to be visited upon an animal part.

DEAD ANIMALS WITH SMOKE

And speaking of food of heroes: In an old *Ren & Stimpy* cartoon, Ren and Stimpy babysat a 400-pound, bearded toddler named Kowalski. Ren: "What to you want to eat, Kowalski?" Kowalski: "MEAT." Ren: "What do you want to drink, Kowalski?" Kowalski: "MEAT."

Marilyn Mach vos Savant, whose IQ measures over 200, was asked by a reader her idea of the ideal food. Her reply: "Anything with the flavor, texture, and nutritional value of meat."

Up until maybe the mid 1600s, "meat" for the English was an idiom for "meal" or "food." They referred to "sitting down to dinner" as "sitting down to meat." This linguistic practice no doubt lasted for hundreds of years.

Allow me to digress: Until the 1600s, English was considered a gutter language by Eurotrash literati. Anyone of English blood, to prove herself sophisticated, learned French. Shakespeare and the King James Version (KJV) of the Bible changed that. Each of these monuments of Western culture contributed probably an equal share to making English a respectable language on the Continent. Until the King James Bible, some of those who translated the Bible into English were executed for it by the English. So a group of scholars approached James, begging his approval of an "official" English translation. Upon being granted that approval, the scholars pieced together the King James version mostly by cannibalizing earlier English versions, selecting sometimes the most poetic things, sometimes the most accurate. Such a story makes me appreciate the beauty of, and dedication and sacrifice represented by, the KJV at the same time that it should give fundamentalists pause regarding whether the KJV is an accurate translation against more recent ones.

But back to meat: Beef gives you zinc, iron (some people report that we get too much iron, so be sure to drink some Italian dry red wine), niacin, potassium, and more. Mainly, it gives you vital complete proteins—combinations of amino acids that allow you to use the protein you eat. You can get complete proteins if you combine whole grains with whole legumes, or if you do some other dietary sleight-of-hand, but why chew laboriously through a giant bowl of beans and rice, as I misguidedly did years ago, when you could get it all from a tiny three-ounce tenderloin? You need some of the fats that come with meat, too, by the way.

A muscular and vigorous vegetarian is possible, but is the rare exception. Most vegans, and I've known a bunch, seem weedy and limp (if strident). College and pro football players eat nearly their weight in steaks monthly. Beef is what's for dinner. Pork is the other white meat. A day without pepper-crusted venison tenderloin is like a day without sunshine. But how to prepare it all, with the modern threats of E. coli, mad cow, and long lines at the best restaurants?

Smoke!

Allow me to digress: Coal- and oil-fired electricity-generating plants are fine with me. Yes, they produce acid rain, but guess what: The polluters are not liable for damage to your property if they're within EPA guidelines and a federal judge decides their polluting is in the public interest. Ain't government great? Another point: If every drug user in the US stopped using drugs today, pushers would voluntarily find other employment tomorrow. If every drug pusher were killed today, they'd all be replaced with new ones tomorrow if the users kept wanting to use drugs. Thus, in principle, unless you generate all of your own electricity from geothermal, wind, or solar, you might as well sue yourself for acid rain. (And if the government would allow us, as individual property owners, to sue polluters, there'd be a lot less acid rain.)

But back to smoke: Borrowing from Alton Brown, the oddball but brilliant TV food scientist, I use a cheap name-brand water smoker designed to hold a charcoal fire in the bottom with a water pan midway between the coals and the meat. The clever part Alton originated is doing away with the fussy charcoal fire—I use two $8.76 Wal-Mart hot plates (hence the above digression into electric power generation) and an iron skillet at the bottom of the smoker, with water-soaked hickory chips in the skillet. My garage smells like Nirvana, probably permanently. (N.B.: I put a candy thermometer next to the meat to make sure the temperature is right.)

You can even use a cheap cut of meat, such as chuck roast. Just salt the outside, if you want an extra-smoky crust, and let it get to room temperature for a bit (I go 15–30 minutes tops), and put into the smoker once the smoker's up to temperature and making lots of smoke. Consult your owner's manual for cooking times, but about 75–90 minutes per pound is probably typical at an inside-the-smoker temperature of around 200 degrees F. Of course, the time depends not only on the weight of the meat, but also on the shape. Play around with it, secure in the knowledge there are basically no bacteria inside the meat (unless it's ground), and tests have shown that even injecting bacteria into the meat is bad for the bacteria. Just don't let the meat dwell at room temperature for too long before smoking. Let the meat rest at room temperature after removing from the smoker, another 20 minutes or so. These instructions will usually yield medium to medium-rare results.

Sauce? You can improvise one better than you can purchase. My basic ingredients are wine, vinegar, black pepper, cayenne pepper, garlic, then butter or cream (if butter, remove from heat before incorporating at the very end). Reduce the sauce until it's little more than a film on the bottom of the pan before adding butter or cream. My last sauce used 4 ounces of shiraz, 4 ounces of kosher blackberry-flavored wine, two ounces of white wine vinegar, a teaspoon of minced garlic, as much black and cayenne pepper as I wanted, and at the end about a tablespoon of butter. Of course, if you make (or buy) your own beef stock or broth, you can reduce that to a thick film ("demiglace") as part of the sauce for an even savorier result.

But with or without sauce, coal-fired electricity, or English-language instructions, just eat yourself some dead animals. With smoke.

BEER

Since I brought it up a few pages back, I ought to flesh out the story of beer. As far as we know for sure, beer predates Babylon at least a little. The Sumerians offered it to their gods, and later Hammurabi mentioned beer in his code of laws—mentioning even the death penalty for transacting for beer improperly, such as with money.

Thus and alas, the history of government meddling in peaceful, voluntary transactions dates back as far as we have records. Beer was exported to Egypt from Babylon, showing that gains from trade also date back as far as we have records. Egyptians experimented with recipes, adding raisins and dates to some of their brews, showing that men who want good food have been striving to make improvements since, well, as long ago as we have records.

While there's no specific mention of beer in the Bible, we can be sure its brewing traveled across the Mediterranean and around it through the Middle East, and probably arose independently in Europe as well. Finding beer "barbaric," Rome tried to replace beer with wine, but since outlying areas didn't always have enough grapes, brewing persisted. Rome even found beer making in Britain, again tried to replace it with winemaking, and again failed.

Beer gained popularity as the population in Europe grew denser (and water supplies grew polluted). Monasteries adopted and improved brewing in the late Dark Ages, which weren't really all that Dark, before 1000 A.D. Beer continued to attract governmental meddling, such as laws that first enabled monasteries to sell beer at their own brewpubs, then later laws forbidding their doing so. The most significant beer law is the German Purity Law of 1516, which mandated that beer be made with only barley, hops, and pure water. Britain outlawed hops during those centuries, then later relented in the face of common sense.

At the time of the Purity Law, it wasn't known that yeast provided fermentation. Brewers, many of whom were working from home, were relying on airborne yeast. The Purity Law was still fully in effect until Germany's incorporation into the European Union effectively negated it as an "unfair trade practice," meaning that little law was observed for almost 500 years. Some German breweries still use only those three ingredients, and proudly note their adherence to the 1516 law on their labels.

Brewing continued its steady improvement until the 19th century, when the improvement accelerated. Watt's steam engine made breweries bigger and more efficient; Louis Pasteur pasteurized beer for the first time (his notes credit beer study with his discoveries regarding microorganisms); refrigeration allowed beer to be brewed year-round, when previously some varieties could be brewed only during cold months; and Christian Hansen discovered that yeast could be cultivated.

In the 20th century, manufacturing methods improved quality, consistency, and sanitation, though until around 1980 mass production (and unfavorable laws) in the US resulted mainly in limited variety. Increasing imports from major breweries and microbreweries from Europe, Central America, and Asia, along with the explosion of microbreweries in the US, has produced what is probably unprecedented variety today. There are over a thousand brewpubs, and at least dozens of microbreweries not attached to pubs, in the US now.

The historical importance of beer for the West can't be overstated. At one time, around 1500 A.D., there were 600 breweries in Hamburg alone. Such concentration was possible because of increased free trade (specialization of labor and all that). Germans at the time were sending beer as far away as India. In fact, the India Pale Ale variety, now a common variant, is based on a British-developed brew that could be exported as far as India without spoiling in the days before refrigeration. Trade by that time was nearly worldwide.

Indeed, even in the mid-1200s, according to unearthed artifacts, Frenchmen knew of over 200 spices, many of which would have come from various places in Asia. How those spices got that far that long ago wasn't known even to some of the middlemen providing them at the time, but everybody made a profit, and everybody was happy with what he got for what he paid.

Alas, not having detailed written history of every culture as we do of Europe is a loss to mankind. We have some sketchy idea that beer developed in South

America hundreds of years ago or longer, and it is probable that beer developed everywhere there was both grain and water. How many recipes have been lost!

That beer has been tremendously important in the lives of men is established by all the records we have. For example, the Code of Hammurabi allowed to wealthy men, and European brewpub monasteries allowed to monks, a ration of 5 liters of beer per day. That would be fourteen 12-ounce bottles. In Germanic lands ca. 1000–1500 A.D., children got two liters per day. Ben Franklin had beer for breakfast, lunch, dinner, and a nightcap.

I don't know how strong beer was in those times and places; some estimates for the alcohol content of ancient Egyptian beer run from 3% by volume to 10%. Given that most brands on the American market today are between 4 and 6%, that most large breweries in America have German lineage, and that the German purity law dates from 1516, it's probably safe to guess that rarely did any beer brewed between 3000 B.C. and today get much lower than 3%. My favorite brewpub has on the menu beers ranging from 4% to 10.5. Ben Franklin and German Dark Aged children were indeed drinking beer.

Now that we have all these choices—what to do? Ah, the glory of capitalism: There are so many good ones available, you can go fat and broke finding a favorite. I've been leaning toward Dutch and German lately; never liked Mexican (except for the Negra Modelo recommended by some of my readers), and can tolerate American megabreweries but prefer some of the micros. Ales, lagers, stouts, pilsners, they're all good.

I have no connoisseur guidelines to offer regarding what sorts of flavors make one beer better than another. If a beer's too bitter or sweet for your liking, then it's no good. I can say that a beer's coming from a micro- or pub brewery doesn't mean it's good. A local brewpub I know uses (or over-roasts) some particular ingredient, making the beer perfectly undrinkable. And any distributor can let beer get too hot in the truck, turning the beer nasty kinds of bitter.

Dedicated brewmasters all over the West have spent the last 1200 years devoting themselves to improving the quality and variety of beers available to us. This legacy more than any other accrues to the work of thousands of poignant and worthy brewmaster lives. To ignore their contributions—to abstain from imbibing of the fruits of their valiant labors—would be dishonorable. Nay!, despicable. Due to the love and labors of unknown, dead, innumerable meisters brewing, we know that liverwurst, beef steak, jalapeno-laden Tex-Mex, and virtually every heroic food known to man reaches its gustatory and visceral zenith only in the presence of beer.

Harken: Hoist!

WHISKEY!

The word "whisky" comes from the Gaelic for "water of life." I can't imagine a more fitting etymology. One online dictionary describes whiskey as a "spirituous liquor distilled from a mash of grains, usually rye, barley, oats, wheat, or corn." Scotland, Ireland, Canada, and the US make the world's whiskey. The only whiskies I care about are from Scotland and Kentucky (about 95% of US whiskey distilleries are in Kentucky) (most of the rest are in Tennessee[9]).

Whiskey—spelled "whisky" in the UK—was made in the Isles at least as far back as the 11th century, in monasteries, no doubt by some of the same heroes who helped develop beer. Whiskey takes a lot of work: First, the grains are malted (allowed to sprout), then fermented. Then they're distilled—simmered to evaporate and collect the alcohol and flavor at a temperature that leaves the water behind. Then the whiskey is aged in wood barrels, usually oak.

The color and flavor you see in the final product are the result of this aging, which takes a minimum of 2 years in Kentucky (law requires that you mention it on the label if you age less than four years), and is done for up to 40 years in some of the most expensive Scotch whiskies. The reason the aging does so much for the whiskey is that somebody burns the inside of the barrel with a blowtorch before using it. This burning produces sugars from the sap in the wood. Resultant ashes and/or soot explain why the whiskey has to be filtered later. New barrels are used for every batch of whiskey in Kentucky,[10] while some used Kentucky barrels are bought and reused by Scottish distillers.

The freshly-distilled, not-yet-aged whiskey is almost as clear as water, relatively flavorless, and 140 to 150 proof. Sometimes the alcohol content is even higher. Whiskey evaporates from the barrels during aging: Up to 25% of the barrel may be lost. After aging, the whiskey is filtered, usually through some variety of carbon, and then bottled. Most whiskey has water added to dilute it to 80 proof (40% alcohol), but some brands offer a variety or two at barrel proof—no water added—which I've seen as high as 126. (Booker's bourbon, aged 7 years. $55 and worth it once in a while.)

---

9.   Jack Daniel, of Jack Daniel's Tennessee Sour Mash Whiskey, died in 1911 at age 61. He couldn't open his office safe, so he kicked it in anger, broke his toe, developed gangrene, and died, ultimately from a tantrum. That wouldn't happen in Kentucky.

10. It's a law. I'm told by readers that this law demonstrates yet another moral hazard of government: It was barrel makers, decades ago, who got this law passed in order to guarantee themselves a living.

So now, you see at least one mechanism that relates longer aging to higher price: Less whiskey remains in the barrel after a longer time, alcohol being the first thing to evaporate; so you're getting more whiskey (barrel) flavor for the bottle. Additionally, more man-hours, barrel years, and grain acres go into a bottle with longer aging.

Scotch whiskies can be blended or single malt. Single malt means the whiskey was made from malted barley at a single distillery; it doesn't necessarily mean grain from a single farm or field. "Blended" means you're getting a blend of whiskies from different malts, possibly from different distilleries, even different manufacturers; and some of the whiskey may be made from unmalted grain. Usually, blends are less expensive, though Johnnie Walker makes one blend that sells for around $200 a bottle. I would never spend that much on a bottle; I've never met a blend I liked.

Bourbon whiskey, a.k.a. Kentucky Straight Bourbon Whiskey, is named for the county in Kentucky whence much of the whiskey once was distributed more than for where the whiskey originates today. To be called "bourbon," the whiskey must be made from at least 51% corn mash, and lesser amounts of other grains. The recipe for the other grains varies from one maker to another.

How do you tell a better whiskey from a bad one by tasting? I have no idea, but I have some ideas: First, there's no such flavor as "smooth," and all whiskies are of the same viscosity and texture (watery), so "smooth" usually will mean only the absence of a bad flavor, or perhaps the presence of a pleasing aftertaste, or "finish," which can take any form.

Many tasting reviews of whiskies and bourbons use such language as "hints of vanilla in the bouquet, peaty and dark on the palate, with a dry oak finish." This is floweredy crapola: Such terms, even if they're accurate, won't tell you whether you like the stuff. You have to taste it yourself.

I am simplifying a bit; Dewar's website[11] will give you names for every particular flavor and aroma that can result from variations in the ingredients, the processing, and the barrels, with terms ranging from "green tomatoes" to "grass cuttings." Copious free time and money are required to develop expertise here, as anywhere. There would be rewards, here, as anywhere.

A few tasting techniques I've learned for chocolate and wine have helped me enjoy good whiskies. First, take a small sip, to ease the sharp bite of the alcohol with your saliva (I know that sounds gross)—most of us can't drink it straight in huge gulps, nor would we want to. With your sinus passages open, holding the

---

11.   http://www.dewars.com/

sip in the front of your mouth, draw in some air and make bubbles, sort of like a reverse gargle. Then wash the whiskey over your entire tongue—the tip, the middle, both sides, all the way to the back. Whether you know anything about whiskey or not, this is a way to taste everything that's there, and to know for sure how much you like the one you're sampling.

Going to all this trouble also makes it take longer to drink too much, and makes it take longer to inure yourself to the flavor (as with the smell of an unfamiliar room once you've been in there a while). Whiskies are complex, and you can discover something new with each of the first several sips.

Once you've tasted a few, you'll find that Scotch single malts and Kentucky bourbons all overlap in flavor, yet they're all different. If you stay away from the cheap stuff (Dixie Dew corn whiskey, 100 proof, is liquid soap), they're all good. There are some families of varieties, such as the Scottish Island single-malt whiskies, all members of which have a peat/iodine flavor, sometimes so strong that it's the only thing you can taste (e.g., a Laphroaig 10-year-old).

After eating a good meal—meat, cheese, salt—there's little I enjoy more than a slice of cheesecake or hunk of chocolate along with a shot of bourbon or single malt. You can even hold the cheesecake and chocolate.

CHOCOLATE

As long as I brought it up: Chocolate has a long and storied history, dating back many centuries and spanning several continents.

Charles Schulz once wrote, in a Peanuts cartoon, "No problem is so big or so complicated it can't be run away from." Well, no food item or tradition is so big or so complicated that I can't confuse things by writing about it. Hence:

Many stories about chocolate, such as ones involving Central or South American kings of antiquity with names like Quatlaccathalthlthlcoatztz drinking up to 50 cups a day of a strong, hot, bitter chocolate drink flavored with oranges and/or hot peppers in the belief that it was an aphrodisiac or potency enhancer or magical longevity elixir, are told.

Scientists today tell us chocolate contains over 200 compounds, some of which have been identified as antioxidants (Magical Cancer Stave-offers); others of which have been found to release pleasure-related neurotransmitters similar, perhaps, to the ones released by tobacco; many of which have not even been identified, much less investigated for their effects.

There are guidelines in the US for the amount of cocoa mass in a gob of chocolate: To be called "chocolate," it's something like 35%, for "milk chocolate" it's something on the order of 10% milk solids, 25% cocoa mass; and so on.

For whatever reason, Europeans seem to have explored candy chocolate-bar flavor possibilities more than Americans. One manufacturer, Hachez, makes a bar that shows 77% cocoa mass on the label (I'm told the EU requires a number on the label). Another, Lindt, has a 70% bar on the market. These are available widely in the US. Remarkably, the 70% bar has more body and bitterness (mmmm…chocolaty bitterness) than the 77% bar. The difference in flavor may be a matter of what beans they buy, or how the beans are processed before being declared "cocoa mass"…

…which highlights the complexity and difficulty of tasting and comparing these things. I'm told the human tongue is good for only four things (tasting-wise): salty, bitter, sour, and sweet. Finer differences in flavor supposedly involve the sense of smell. That explains why inhaling and exhaling gently with the nose and mouth together when tasting something complex and worthwhile, like chocolate or whiskey, makes sense.

Add to that what must be inherent differences among individuals in the precise ways their tongue and nose cells communicate with brain centers (where the taste sensation really happens), and things get more complicated. Further, if you've French-kissed more than one person in your life, you know different people…um…taste different. We all make our own saliva, and we all must have different balances of enzymes and biowhatnottery in there. I understand we carry permanent biological signatures in our mouths of everyone we've ever French-kissed. Add to that the importance of memory—training—in tasting, and by now things are so complicated that nobody can say anything about how anything tastes to anybody.

That being said, chocolate is good.

But don't try to make your own chocolate confection from raw beans unless you're (a) independently wealthy, (b) a chemist, and (c) retired. You have to ferment, dry, roast, alkalize, drain, treat, separate, and do all kinds of things to the beans, things the likes of which make it amazing that it was all discovered by people with ante-Beverly Hillbillian technology. The important byproducts are cocoa mass (a.k.a. chocolate) and cocoa butter, which you then have to mix back together to make a chocolate bar.

If you're going to make your own chocolate bars from scratch, the scratchiest you'd want to get is buying cocoa mass and cocoa butter separately. As an alternative, in the baking section of your local grocery you can find unsweetened baking chocolate bars. Ingredients: "chocolate." The only disadvantage is that you aren't in control of the cocoa mass-cocoa butter ratio. Then again, unless you're in the industry, you're not in charge of how the beans were roasted, when they were alkalized (before vs. after roasting), etc. But you still have lots of control over the result.

Just for the educational benefit, take a bite of that 100% chocolate bar. Chew thoroughly, and wash it all over your tongue. This will tell you it's a good ingredient, but not a good final product. It's so bitter it's not even fun.

So, to make your own confection, you need only three to five ingredients: chocolate (or cocoa mass and cocoa butter); a sweetener; some vanilla flavoring; and maybe an emulsifier. Lecithin is the most common emulsifier, and you can find it in granular, powder, and liquid forms in your local Tattooed Lesbian Vegetarian Health Food Store. The biggest factor you control is the sweetener: which one, and how much. I've used maple syrup and honey so far, but have big plans to try confectioner's sugar once, and blackstrap molasses more than once.

As to methodology, if you watch the food.tv.whatever shows, you'll end up with double-boilers and whisks and whatever and a messed-up kitchen. I am an Oscar Madison bachelor, so my kitchen's messed up right now, and will be the next time I set to work on a homemade chocolate bar. Therefore, I use a bowl and a fork. Break up the 100% chocolate bar into the bowl. Pour in some vanilla flavoring (or scrapings from the inside of a vanilla bean). Add sweetener. Put the bowl in the oven at 150 degrees and go do something else. When you remember later that it's in the oven, get it out and stir it up with the fork. Let it cool on top of the stove. When you remember later that the bowl's there, put it in the fridge with some plastic wrap over the top. Sample it tomorrow.

The objective of this is that soon you'll know how much of which ingredients will make the best chocolate in the world for you.

I'm also thinking of trying powdered coffee, powdered tea, and garlic as ingredients. (Don't laugh about the garlic; I did it once years ago, and she liked it.) Other ingredients nobody mentions, but that ought to be considered, are powdered cayenne pepper, dehydrated carrots, dehydrated tomatoes, and whatever else you can think of. Maybe hard Italian cheese. Do these one at a time, though—make one bar with the carrot flakes, one with dried apricot, etc. Don't try adding carrots and garlic at the same time until you've tried each one separately. Orange, raspberry, nuts, etc. have already been done, but they haven't been done by you under conditions where you control the sweetness and bitterness, so don't rule anything out.

I don't know offhand of any wars fought over chocolate, any government grants of monopolies to chocolatiers, or government attempts to control chocolate distribution (aside from the little EU law, but that's par for the government food-meddling course). Perhaps the only thing to be learned from chocolate is that you can make it more to your liking than you can find it in the store, and mess only one dish in the process.

We already know that for most of us, chocolate is delicious, addictive, fancy; there's almost no time when we wouldn't like a bite (experiment on your spouse—wake her up in the middle of the night by waving a piece under her nose, see what results); and we now have the plausible scientific claim that it's good for us. Enjoy.

HOT SAUCE

Chocolate always makes me think of hot sauce. There must be around 2.3 bazillion hot sauces on the market now. They all sell just as fast as manufacturers can make them. Why is hot sauce so compelling? Why is hot sauce an excellent exemplar of entrepreneurship? These are the questions that strike the inquiring mind very late on a Sunday evening, when your author is staying up as if to postpone the start of the workweek.

Why hot sauce is so desirable is unknown. Chemical or spice heat in food is nothing more than pain, pure and simple. Unlike salt, which serves as an electrolyte to help make foods taste more like themselves, hot sauce adds only a mouth feel, usually one unrelated to the flavors of the food it's used on. Whether there could be an evolutionary advantage to enjoying spicy foods I don't know—I can't think of one. Chemical heat doesn't occur naturally in any of the other major food groups: Meat, grains and nuts, meat, dairy, and meat.

Perhaps hot foods stimulate the thrill-seeker in some of us. Strangely, a tolerance for hot foods is like some other popular individual differences in that it has no relation to any other observable aspects of a person's physique. Additionally, tolerance for chemical heat in food seems to be completely unrelated to thrill-seeking proclivity, in my unscientifically recorded personal experience.

Whatever the reason, we find it compelling. I, for one, can't imagine a complete meal that doesn't involve meat, heat, salt, and sweet. The compelling nature of food heat has brought more entrepreneurs, and more attendant lessons, out of the woodwork than cellular phones and high-speed Internet connections have.

Hot sauces and hot foods are now available in pain levels from "mild" to "XXX." Just so you know, XXX hot sauces provide almost no flavor at all—nothing but pain, even for seasoned (pardon the pun) hot-sauce competition judges. The XXX stuff is made with pure capsaicin, extracted and concentrated from hot peppers.

There is pretty much the one classic—Tabasco sauce, from Avery Island, Louisiana. The original recipe is very hot, but has plenty of flavor. It's perfect for vegetable soup, cheese and crackers, and all manner of junk food. I've been known to put it on bittersweet chocolate, though the vinegar flavor doesn't always work well. For chocolate bars, I recommend powdered cayenne pepper.

Tabasco presents some important lessons to entrepreneurs. First, there's quality: The Tabasco folks take about three years to produce a bottle of their original hot sauce. Peppers are aged for most of that time. Second, there's name recognition. Through being the first on the block, and spending big money on merchandising (the well-dressed man must have at least one Tabasco necktie), Tabasco is the first thing reached for by people who don't know much about hot sauce. It's the standard.

Third, there's product development. Tabasco, in recent years, has offered a slew of new hot sauces. Their green sauce has gone through at least two recipe changes; and they now offer a habanero sauce (not actually as hot as the original Tabasco), a chipotle sauce, a garlic sauce, and hot jellies. Since they keep coming up with recipes, there is no doubt they believe that offering a range is more profitable than offering a single product. And since the Tabasco company is the champ, their intuitions are generally worth noting.

Finally, there's the important lesson that most entrepreneurs don't make a hit with every single idea. For example, the recipe changes to the green sauce imply that earlier recipes weren't successful. The neckties and coffee mugs are proof Tabasco has hired some marketing folks who've told them to diversify in order to exploit brand recognition. Finally, if you look at their online store, you'll find many stupid items nobody would want, such as sauce-bottle holders and carrying racks. Some of these items represent low risk in that they probably cost pennies to produce, and many will probably soon disappear, only to be replaced with Tabasco-branded silverware and underwear folders. No matter; the cash cow—the original sauce—will carry the Tabasco folks through the experimental successes and failures. I always have at least one bottle of the original sauce on hand along with one of the experimental sauces.

Another lesson for entrepreneurs is that no market should be viewed as saturated if you're better than the next guy. Human wants and needs are inexhaustible. No matter how efficient manufacturing becomes, there is room for new entrepreneurs in any remotely free market. For example, Dave, of Dave's Insanity Sauces, the driving force behind the XXX movement, came from nowhere. He began by making sauces only for his local market. Now, he's international, making as much and expanding as fast as he can.

Thus does mankind move forward, improving our standard of living as surely and doggedly as the sun rises. It isn't just the scientists in the big factories and research centers who improve our lives. Anyone with an idea, a recipe, or a backyard vegetable garden is at risk of hitting the big time. All that's needed is a little ambition and cleverness. Anytime there's something on the market people enjoy and want to buy, there's an opportunity for you and me to get rich.

And these opportunities aren't always obvious. Nobody would have envisioned Coca-Cola 200 years ago, though someone could have made it then, just as they could've made Tabasco back then. You don't need 21st century technology, though the technology enhances productivity and sanitation by leaps and bounds. There's always room for entrepreneurs to create wealth, and to become wealthy for having done it.

EAT FAT

Your local supermarket is full of low-fat this, reduced-fat that, and nonfat the other thing. Advertisements, self-help books, most diet books, a few alarmist MDs, and a million infomercials tell you that fat is the disease, and not eating fat (or burning it more efficiently) is the cure. The word must get out: Fat is delicious, and unless your doctor tells you otherwise based on familiarity with your body and circumstances, reasonable doses of it won't kill you.

Professional bodybuilders, much of the medical community, and others have known for a while that ultra-low-fat diets, unless prescribed by a physician, may not do you any good. A balance of 40-30-30 (40% of calories from carbohydrates, the more complex the better; 30% each from protein and fat) is at least as good, better for many people, than 70-20-10. The trick: If your body detects too little fat in the diet, it makes its own fat out of carbohydrates. The 30% fat ratio satisfies the body's need and tells it there's no famine. Note, however, that it is assumed that you are physically active—if you lead a sedentary enough life, you can be a tub on a low-calorie diet, regardless of carbohydrate-protein-fat breakdown.

In cooking, fat helps you taste the food by fixing flavors better to the tongue (I don't have proof of this; a famous chef said it, and I believe him). Fat improves the texture of food in various and wonderful ways—aside from making sauces richer, more luxurious, and more satisfying, it makes potato chips, and anything else you can deep fry, crispier. Try any baked potato or nacho chips, and you'll see what I mean.

Further, caveat emptor: Some of those low- and non-fat items at the grocery store come from nutritional outer space. Read the labels on margarine, as some versions of it are far worse for you than whole butter. Make sure it's 100% vegetable oil, if you must use margarine (which, for the chef, is good for nothing). And as for those snacks with fat substitutes, if a label says "overconsumption may have a laxative effect" or something equally ominous, you can bet it's true. Nobody eats five potato chips. So if you're a normal person, and eat half a bag of those fat-substitute potato chips at once, your routine will be interrupted at some time in the near future.

How to use fat to its best advantage? Two brilliant applications come to mind. Here's how to make a roux, a great thickener for soups, stews, sauces, and gumbo: Put equal amounts of whole butter and flour into a sauté pan, on medium to medium-low heat. Have a beer handy (for drinking purposes only), because making a roux takes time. Stir and cook until browned—the darker the better for some recipes, though a lighter roux will retain more thickening power than a darker one. You do want to at least cook out all the floury taste. Once it's a bit brown, taste it (warning! It's murderously hot—get some on a spoon, and cool it a whole lot before tasting). You'll be amazed at the palate-swathing luxury of plain ol' butter and flour together.

A second application: sautéing in clarified butter and olive oil. Get a pan hot, and put in equal amounts of clarified butter and extra-virgin olive oil. Then throw in a diced onion. The aroma of the fats alone will make you think you've gone to heaven; adding the onion will make you think a great chef followed you there.

Low-fat foods and diets are hip because the food nannies never sleep. And now they've enlisted lawyers. Movie-theater popcorn, Chinese takeout, cheeseburgers, undercooked eggs—there is no American gustatory delicacy beyond their alarmist reach. They will never stop until they're ignored. To rebel, eat some or all of the following, and drive up the demand for fat. (Disclaimer: Ask somebody who knows something before making any of the below a daily item in your diet.)

Beef Filets with Extra Fat

Find the best-looking Angus filets you can. Broil, to caramelize the outside nicely, and cook to a medium rare. The trick: Don't use meat thermometers or cut the meat open; just mash gently with a knife blade or fork, and you'll be able to tell how done the filets are. Another trick: If you broil, place the filets on a trivet, so they don't boil in—and out—their juices. Let rest for 15 minutes before eating, so the juices fix within the meat, and you won't have a plate full of blood and dry meat.

For a sauce, dice some onion, bacon, and fresh jalapeno; mash some garlic; slice some mushrooms; and sauté the whole mélange in clarified butter and olive oil (remember to add the garlic at the very end, so as not to scorch it). Deglaze with red wine and beef stock, and reduce until it thickens a bit, or thicken with a little roux.

For presentation, spoon the sauce over the filets, then add a thin slice of extra-sharp cheddar cheese over the top. Life is good. Hoard Tums®.

New York Strip with Eggs

Find the best-looking New York Strip steaks you can. Broil to medium rare.

Dice a strip of bacon and render in a hot pan; remove the bacon and fry eggs to your preferred degree of doneness in the bacon fat. Place the bacon and eggs on the steaks. If you must, grate some extra-sharp cheddar cheese over the top. For a dipping sauce, reduce beef stock and red wine with a few splashes of balsamic vinegar; add plenty of butter, and a little corn starch to keep the butter from separating. A trick: Make a cold slurry of the cornstarch with red wine, remove the sauce from the heat, and add the slurry slowly while stirring the sauce; keep stirring as you reapply the heat. You'll get a professional result. Or, again, use a roux.

If you use a good bit of the vinegar, you won't need the Tums®.

Other Valve-Snapping Ideas

- Add pepperoni slices to any meaty tomato sauce.

- For a pasta sauce, try extra-virgin olive oil, clarified butter, diced bacon, sliced black olives, cayenne pepper, and black pepper. Add parmesan cheese at presentation. Keep in mind that you don't need the pasta overwhelmed by the sauce; just lightly coated is enough.

- For a salad, toss together a variety of dark greens along with some radicchio. For the dressing, use a few splashes of balsamic vinegar and red wine vinegar. Then dice two strips of bacon and render. Pour the bacon and a little of the grease over the top of the salad. Add grated cheese.

- Learn to cook with lard.

There's no placing limits on the culinary mind. Someday, somewhere, you'll meet up with a real-life fat nanny, and there's only one good response: Share one of these recipes, or a similar one of your own; share how much you enjoy it; recommend they try it. Disobedience can be its own reward. Please reread the disclaimer above.

But seriously, do everything sensibly and in moderation. Fortunately, moderation means enjoying everything. Good, plain, old-fashioned fat ought to be right around 30% of "everything." Tell the alarmists to go bother somebody else.

LIBERTY GARDENING

Our government has a stranglehold on the food industry, via wrongheaded and burdensome regulations such as those that require apple growers to file federal forms proving they've trained their workers in the use of goggles; via farm subsidies that inhibit competition and reward sloth, with some farmers being paid six-figure salaries to leave fields fallow, making us pay higher prices so "farmers" can watch daytime television full-time; via taxes at every stage of production; and finally through expensive and ineffective inspection programs that allow E. coli contaminated meat onto the market, to be recalled with haste following the first few dozen poisonings. Without government involvement, you can be assured our food supply would be cheaper, more abundant, more varied, and safer than it is now.

Mostly because they enjoy the activity itself, but partly in order to avoid government as much as possible, many southerners naturally turn to hunting. The government still has its say, of course: You have to apply for a permit to hunt and the government tells you where and when you can hunt, what weapon you can use, and how much you can kill. The effective anti-government response would be to raise your own livestock, which of course is impractical for most of us; or simply for landowners to allow other folks to hunt for a fee. This happens already, and successfully, in Texas and all over Europe. For the time being, however, the rest of us are stuck with oppressive hunting regulations, or more oppressive (but more accessible) grocery-store meat gathering.

Vegetables offer a tiny bit of an escape. Vegetables you grow in your own yard, or even in the house, will tend to be tastier and more nutritious than those you get from the grocery store, mostly because they're fully vine-ripened and fresher. I've grown gorgeous yellow bell peppers that splash juice at you when you cut them, and zucchini the size of a football. Further, aside from the sales tax you pay on seeds or seedlings, there are only weak regulations (such as neighborhoods not allowing you to grow tall corn in the front yard), or none at all, on how much you can grow and eat. And fresh vegetables, loaded with vitamins and minerals, keep the mind as clear as it can be, an asset for devising ways to expand and protect your liberty.

Growing your own vegetables saves money. Furthermore, a backyard gardener can be extraordinarily productive. Many folks with less than a quarter acre under till give away baskets of surplus food every August and September, at least here in the south. Certainly, such behavior, spread around the neighborhood, fosters friendship and a sense of community. Not to be ignored is the tax loss to the government that would result if all of us were to grow more of our own food and pass it around. Even if the loss would be small, it would be pleasing. It gives new meaning to the term "victory garden."

You can't live by grains and vegetables alone. Your body wants plenty of meat, cheese, and eggs. Use unsalted butter on them. But just to give you ideas of what to plant, here are a couple of recipes that make use of vegetables you can grow in your back yard:

Corn: Sauté, in clarified butter and extra-virgin olive oil: diced onion, jalapeno, bell pepper, and fresh black pepper. If you're going to use salt, add it at the beginning. Deglaze with a splash of dry white wine. Add cut yellow corn (if you don't grow your own, use fresh or frozen—avoid canned corn). When cooked to your satisfaction, add grated extra-sharp cheddar cheese, fresh cilantro, and flat-leaf parsley. Stir and serve.

Black beans: Sauté diced onion, jalapeno, and black pepper. Add some cumin seed—crush it by hand or run it through a coffee grinder. Deglaze with dry white wine, then add black beans. Simmer (adding, and occasionally sipping, the wine as required) for 20 minutes or so. To thicken, mash some of the beans with a fork and stir. At presentation, add grated Monterey Jack or white American cheese, and flat-leaf parsley. Add some fresh oregano if you have it. Don't try to grow beans yourself unless you want to go to that kind of trouble. Canned black beans are fine, unless you know how to deal with dried ones.[12]

These two dishes are great together, especially when served with a nice beef filet. To make it really luxurious, slap a fried egg or my marinara sauce on top of the filet. Serve with plenty of beer (you can brew that at home, too) and conversation.

But whatever it takes, grow your own food. Till, plow, seed, weed, harvest, eat, and live gustatory autonomy. Get the government out of your kitchen, mouth, and wallet as much as you can. You'll be healthier and happier.

LOBSTERPIECE

No list of good foods and recipes, whether intended as political object-lessons or not, would be complete without some discussion of lobster. Not all of the lobster's lessons are political, but they are at least earthy:

First, since you should always eat lobster that's been alive and kicking up until cooking time, preparing lobster at home returns you to the primeval essence of eating other animals. Those of us who don't have the time or inclination to go off hunting still can appreciate—not in the entertainment sense, mind you, but in the dust-to-dust sense—first-hand contact with the food chain and the life cycle. From an old cookbook: Kill the lobster "by inserting a sharp knife in the shell where the body and tail meet and severing the spinal cord." Then you turn him over and split him open while his body is oftentimes still wiggling. (Hey, remember—it wasn't 100 years ago when most families killed their own chickens at home.) The lessons: We're not all intended to share the planet as if we're on some equal moral footing. Food critters are here for us to enjoy. And good cooking isn't always for the squeamish.

Second, though this isn't as much of an object lesson, lobsters are closely related to cockroaches on the species tree. This means that food doesn't have to be intelligent (or make a good pet) to be delicious. It also means that the lobster doesn't really know he's on death's door when he's on your cutting board. Perhaps the knife method is more humane than the boiling method of killing him, but neither takes much time.

---

12. Put dried beans and enough tap water to cover the beans by a couple of inches, at room temperature, into a pot. Bring to a boil and boil for three minutes. Turn off the heat, and let rest for a few hours. Drain and rinse, then cook. This avoids the overnight-soaking step, though it produces beans that fall apart easier. It's still a pain, so I use canned beans.

As to political lessons, the television chef Bobby Flay recently visited lobster fishermen and restaurants in Maine (where lobster's so cheap, you can buy it on a hot dog bun with mayo). He learned there are laws governing what sizes and sorts of lobsters the fishermen can keep. This sort of law wouldn't need to arise if the lobster-fishing waters were private property. Property owners who wanted to preserve the lobster population would make their own rules, and lease fishing rights to fishermen individually. Contracts would specify what the fishermen could do, and you can bet individual property owners would write better rules than the government.

Flay also learned that 200 years ago, lobsters were considered peasant food. Since they weren't much in demand, anyone could walk in ankle-deep water along the Maine coast and catch as many as he wanted. That's the sort of bounty we'd see if property were private. But since the fishing waters are considered public property, the fishermen have to be monitored by the government so the lobster population isn't fished down to nothing. People in Maine who don't eat, fish for, or care about lobster have to foot the bill for all this regulation and enforcement, when the lobster fishermen, lobster water owners, and lobster eaters should be the only ones affected.

And now, in case you need any encouragement to cook lobster at home, here's a recipe:

Lobster Edmonds
(Lobster with garlic grits in orange sauce)

Pot 1: Boil the lobsters in white wine, vegetable broth, and orange juice—no water. (An entirely reasonable shortcut for vegetable broth would be to use those vegetable bullion cubes in the green and yellow boxes at the grocery. But be careful about adding any salt when you use one of those.) After the lobsters have blushed, remove the meat, discard the organs, and put the shells back into the same pot to simmer. From now on, keep this pot uncovered; the liquid has some reducing to do. You may need to simmer at a pretty high speed to reduce the liquid to your satisfaction in a reasonable amount of time.

Pot 2: Put the lobster meat in this pot with at least a bunch of unsalted, clarified butter. Let cook on low heat, or better, just warm through as you're ready to plate the dish. You don't want the lobster to overcook and toughen, but you do want it fully cooked. At least I do.

Pot 3: Sauté *roughly cut* carrots, leeks, and jalapenos. When they've browned a bit, put them in Pot 1 with the lobster shells and liquid. Then deglaze Pot 3 with a splash of white wine to get any brown stuff off the bottom of the pan, and add that to Pot 1 also. Then, back in pot 3, sauté *finely diced* carrots, leeks, celery, and jalapeno.

Be sure to adjust the jalapeno heat level to your liking. Jalapenos can vary considerably in this regard. Start with less than you'll need, then add as necessary. Even if you can take a lot of pepper heat, it wouldn't be fitting for it to dominate this dish.

Pot 4: Sauté four or more whole cloves of garlic in extra-virgin olive oil (crush the cloves once, but leave them intact). Keep the oil temperature moderate, to avoid scorching the garlic. When the oil has taken on a lot of the garlic flavor and aroma, remove the garlic cloves and save them for the garlic bread; cook grits in this pot with this oil, according to instructions on the package.

Finish: Strain and discard the vegetables and shells from the liquid in Pot 1; add the liquid to the sautéing vegetables in Pot 2; deglaze with whatever liquid is handy (as long as it's not water). Thicken with cornstarch, whole butter, or a little roux. This is now the orange sauce. On each plate, put a serving of the grits in the center, and place pieces of the lobster meat on top and around. Spoon the orange sauce all around the grits. Garnish with fresh Italian parsley and grated orange zest.

For spectacular garlic bread, use the butter left from cooking the lobster, and the garlic cloves you sautéed in the olive oil. Mash the cloves and butter into a paste with a spoon and some salt, or just rub the garlic cloves onto the bread and then spread the oil onto the bread with a brush. Crack some black pepper on top, and maybe grate a little Romano cheese over it as well. Pass the bread under a broiler to brown.

Grits, by the way, are called "polenta" in Italy, and you can get the typical fashion-conscious American city dweller to spend five times as much for polenta as grits would cost. Then he'll slave in the kitchen over it, smug in the knowledge that he's enjoying exotic cuisine. Don't tell him it's just grits.

There need be no further proof than any good lobster dish that food animals were put here for our pleasure. "Stewardship" means making sure there are plenty of them to eat, and that they're as healthy, fresh, and affordable as they can be. And we've seen all over the world that when an animal fetches a good price, and merchants have property rights to the critter and/or its habitat, it's never in danger of extinction (as is the case with any commodity that's in demand, especially all the illegal ones).

BUGS

As long as we're talking about lobster: Apparently, you can find, maybe once or twice a year, a bug-eating festival somewhere in North America. Crickets, ants, beetles, and some insects that look to me like large outdoor cockroaches are stir-fried and eaten by actual people at these festivals. Some of these people toss live, struggling mealworms right into their mouths and crunch away.

Also apparently, Americans shouldn't be horrified by this. While I've always known that bugs are nutritious, it seems North America is the only continent where bugs aren't eaten routinely. Fortunately (?), a quick web search will provide plenty of results with information about the techniques and joys of bug eating.

Think of the implications of bug cuisine. There are hundreds of species of bugs that are already known to be safe, nutritious, and tasty. There are probably tens of thousands of additional species, mostly untested or unrecorded, that would be suitable as food for people. Bugs are everywhere, they're difficult to eradicate as pests, and so far nobody's jumping to their defense (PETB instead of PETA?). Given bug behavior and the size of the bug brain, it seems fair to presume that bugs fear death and pain less than mammals. Surely it seems less like murder to the squeamish when a bug is eaten than when we butcher a lively, intelligent pig.

Further, given the hardiness and the sheer numbers of bugs, they should constitute a reliable, renewable, high-protein food source for developing countries with population problems. Here's the nutritional breakdown for 100 grams (a little under four ounces) of crickets:

> 121 calories, 12.9 grams of protein, 5.5 g. of fat, 5.1 g. of carbohydrates, 75.8 mg. calcium, 185.3 mg. of phosphorous, 9.5 mg. of iron, 0.36 mg. of thiamin, 1.09 mg. of riboflavin, and 3.10 mg. of niacin.[13]

There are yet more advantages to eating bugs: You can raise your own—lots of them—in a small space, very small compared to the space required for raising, say, beef cattle. Bugs don't require acres of grassland that the eco-nazis think should be devoted to wildlife (and themselves). Bugs don't emit the greenhouse gases cattle emit, and I've never heard of an E. coli or trichinosis outbreak associ-

---

13.   Here's a page with links about bug cuisine, nutrition information, recipes, and more: http://www.creepycrawlycuisine.150m.com/msg5.htm.

ated with eating bugs (though you do want to at least wash them before eating, and avoid urban street bugs because they might be covered in pesticides). And finally, I can't think of a more satisfying or amusing picture than a bunch of Sierra Clubbers and PETAns sitting around the campfire eating handfuls of roaches and beetles. (A campfire, by the way, makes more greenhouse gases than does a giant new SUV—big SUVs are 96.3% clean for hydrocarbon compared to passenger cars of the 1960s[14].)

Whether bugs could be part of gourmet cuisine or not (the snail-eating French would say yes), they are a food of survival and optimism. As a food source, bugs teach us two important lessons. First, they remind us once again that human overpopulation is greatly exaggerated.[15] Not only are we producing more food per person worldwide than we were 40 years ago (with the lone exception of Africa), we're doing it at a lower cost and at a higher level of productivity per acre. Thank machinery, chemicals, and genetic engineering for that; and thank individuals and capitalism for these things, not government (which, as we've seen, pays farmers to destroy crops). And this big rosy food outlook is the case even though we in North America have completely ignored bugs as a viable, plentiful, and cheap food source. The second lesson: Um...gustatory splendor is in the eye of the beholder. Never consider an aesthetic judgment to be written in stone.

Of course, once we start eating bugs in large numbers, we'll have PETA types spraying grocery-store arachnid managers with silly string; and as soon as we genetically engineer some golden crickets with carotene that might help prevent child blindness in the far east, we'll have leftist hippie activists burning down bug engineering labs. The media will make headlines of predictions that giant mutant bugs will do terrible things to us. We'll have to cross those bridges when we come to them.

In the meantime, explore entomophagy (bug eating). At the very least, it'll change your thinking about food. I'll let you try it first, and you can tell me about it.

---

14.   Pat Bedard, *Car and Driver*, July 2000.
15.   For example, the entire world population (6.1 billion right now), if jammed into the state of Texas, would reach the population density of Washington, DC. You can run the numbers yourself with an ordinary road atlas and a pocket calculator.

More Bugs

We've already been eating worms!

While pouring out some cat food not long ago, I noticed white mold holding the niblets together. Closer inspection revealed there were also dead, dry, 3/8"-long, beige, ringed worms in there. All through the box. After ascertaining that my cat, Casey, seemed okay (she had already eaten some over the preceding 24 hours), I tried to call the company. Alas, their customer service line is open only 7 hours a day.

So, I sent The Company (its initials are Purina) an email. I then had to leave the house to buy more cat food—poor Casey was hungry. On the drive, I entertained fantasies of writing an exposé that would make me famous, perhaps land me a steady talking-head gig on national television. I took the box to the grocery store manager, giving him the whole story regarding why I wanted a new box but needed to keep the old one as evidence. The manager was quite knowledgeable about food, as is fortunate considering his occupation, and he explained it this way:

In almost any grain product, there are worm eggs. I don't remember what the worms are called. If there's a little heat, and enough time, worms may begin hatching. The box I held had been purchased a week prior, and I had noted its expiration date. Other boxes on the shelf had expiration dates around six months later, meaning my box was six months older than the others, though its expiration date was still months away. My box could have been subjected to the necessary heat in the back of the truck that delivered it.

Did I say almost *any* grain product? Yes: The manager did me the dubious favor of showing me some spaghetti, in packages on the shelf. "See those teeny tiny black dots?" Some percentage of those dots are the same sort of worm eggs. Joy.

The Purina story I got back was a little different: Since Cat Chow is baked, no viable worm eggs could survive (of course, Purina denied there were any worm eggs upon packaging, though the spaghetti example seems to suggest otherwise). Thus, any worms that developed in the package must have come from an invasion in transit. I am persuaded that worm eggs wouldn't survive the baking. Both stories are probably correct, and both seem necessary (though I'm not a worm-egg scientist) to account for all the data too familiar with which I've now become.

Purina probably had nothing to do with my wormy cat food, and surely didn't do anything wrong. What's more, the worm cocktail is generally harmless—these worms aren't parasites; consider them something like Klingon food—and has been shown through daily, universal, accidental experimentation to be pretty much harmless to people as well. Note, however, this is NOT a suggestion that you store your pasta unwrapped in the garage for a year before using it. Try the fridge instead.

So my big exposé fizzled. I'll stick with Purina Cat Chow because of the low cost compared to some premium cat foods, and to avoid the carpet hazard of changing a cat's diet. (Cats love to throw up. Casey does it almost gleefully: "See what I did to your carpet? Wasn't that fun?") I will keep a closer eye on her food when I pour, and now I'll also be visually inspecting my pasta for movement. (Some years ago, I kept rice in an airtight container in a cabinet, and when I opened it there was movement. Maybe keep your rice in the fridge, too.)

Oh, and: Boil your pasta.

4

Lessons From the Market

We've examined some of the things government does, some of the things markets do, and the results as they apply to our stomachs and our wallets. Being part of the market for most of us means being a producer during the day, and a shopper in the evenings and on weekends. We haven't looked yet at food production—market participation—from the producer's perspective. This perspective is useful, though, since you may produce food yourself someday (if you aren't already), and because the perspective is illustrative in its own right.

LEARNING THE WRONG LESSONS FROM THE MARKET

A group of apparently unwitting entrepreneurs calling themselves Slow Food[1] (as opposed to fast food, I guess) has created an "endangered species" list of foods from around the world. These foods have in common only that they are rare. Most are regional specialties, such as some particularly huge oysters from the Atlantic coast and black-cherry wine from Italy. Slow Foods hopes to promote the endangered foods, which they expect will increase demand, which would result in increasing production and availability of the foods.

This suggests one of two things about the economic education of those involved: Either they've had a lot of it, or they've had none at all. Among the foods they're promoting are the above-mentioned black cherry wine and certain specific varietal fruits. Being specific to a region, such products (especially fresh fruits and vegetables) are in season only at certain times, and are expensive due to limited production. Hence, the market is extinguishing these items, extinguish-

---

1. The Fox News story was still available on the web as of May, 2004 at
   http://www.foxnews.com/story/0%2C2933%2C64587%2C00.html.

ing them at least from broader distribution, because there are other items that do the job better—similar fruits that are available year-round, or are produced by major agribusinesses and therefore far less expensive.

In fact, a quote from one of the Slow Food leaders shows the possible dumb-headedness of the thinking behind the movement: "We are attempting to rescue products that are in danger of dying out because there's no market for them." If "no market" means people don't want the items, the movement is doomed, as are the particular foods. If nobody wants a particular kind of wine, then nobody cares if it disappears (except the guy making the wine, and he just needs to go into another line of business). If "no market" means only that people haven't heard of the products, well, then once they've heard of them, there will be a market *if* the products are somehow superior.

The latter point is where Slow Foods may be getting it right: Perhaps the foods they list are truly superior, and it is almost assured that once they are publicized they'll be in high demand. This will indeed rescue the foods from extinction, since (as any economist knows) high demand will create production by giving entrepreneurs an incentive to produce.

This is true even in the most extreme cases, as for example high demand for cocaine keeps creating growers and distributors, many of whom are deliberately erroneously called "pushers" when in fact their activities are pulled by the demand of the market.

If people begin demanding farm-made raw-milk Edam cheese, farmers will begin producing it, and this special cheese will be saved from extinction. If Slow Foods is aware of this, then their economic thinking is better than that of the US government…

…which brings us back to Slow Foods' possible errors. In some cases, such as oysters found only in a certain bay, it may not be possible to increase production, and Slow Foods' publicizing the delicacy may lead to a spike in harvesting (depending on laws governing the bay) and permanent disappearance of the delicacy. In other cases, such as raw-milk Edam cheese, given the higher sanitary standards that must be observed, the product might remain very expensive regardless of increases in production, while imitators in Wisconsin might produce something just as good, if not identical, in flavor for a price so much lower that the real thing could never catch on.

As an example, Wisconsin's very good imitations of parmesan cheese cost $6/lb, while the real thing is $19/lb. The real thing is lovely, but not three times as lovely as the imitation; and the real thing will remain a niche item forever as long as the price is so high. In still other cases, it is possible that the market just doesn't want the thing. Fish heads are a delicacy in Japan, but probably never will catch on in the US, regardless how they're promoted or how available and affordable they might become. Thus, it is possible that some of the items on the endangered food list are disappearing because they really *should* disappear.

Any time you can try something new in a good restaurant, and that new thing doesn't sound repulsive to you (i.e., there's a chance you'll really enjoy it), consider it. The same goes for grocery shopping. But always evaluate the claims of new gurus, such as Slow Foods, critically. I intend to peruse their list of delicacies, if I can find it, but I'm also going to consider price, availability, and whether I want a thing in the first place before I plan a menu around it or even spend a dime helping prevent its disappearance from the market.

After all, you already can produce spectacular dishes of your own with perfectly common ingredients. We have seen this already with Walnut Chili, marinated white grapes with fettuccini Alfredo, lobster with grits…

LEARNING THE RIGHT LESSONS FROM THE MARKET

There are food entrepreneurs who aren't ignorant of market forces. According to a news item that made the rounds not long ago, researchers have found a new way to slice tough parts of the cow normally reserved for hamburger. The important part of this news is that the new cuts produce steaks competitive in flavor and texture with traditional cuts that cost twice as much per pound. Restaurant customers have made the new cuts, where available, the most popular items on the menu. This says so many things about free markets that I almost don't know where to begin.

First, I'm reminded of the "noble savage." Among the worshipful mantras bandied about in praise of American Indians by leftists are that they used every part of each buffalo they killed. This was noble because it minimized the number of buffalo necessary to kill, it expressed reverence for mama earth and her happy critters, and so on.

Frankly, it isn't so noble when you think about it: It's easier, in a pre-industrial setting, to make clothing from animal skin than from cotton. And as long as you have the bones, you might as well make tools and weapons, rather than hunting for the perfect rock for every tool. And it's easier to keep cutting meat from the animal you killed, even if it's relatively unpalatable, than to kill another animal. (Still and all, you might as well know that on those occasions when they ran a herd of buffalo off a cliff, the average tribe would get far more buffalo than they could eat. The vast majority of the kill had to be left to rot.)

At any rate, with the help of science and modern production technologies, motivated by the competitiveness of the open market, we've more than caught up with the noble savage in our comprehensive use of the cow. And the noble savage proves our equal in recognizing the natural disutility of labor. (Side note: The "natural disutility of labor" doesn't mean we're all lazy; it means if we see two ways of meeting the same goal, and one way is more efficient than the other, we use the more efficient method. It would be stupid to do otherwise.)

Also, we're demonstrating a well-established trend that's only recently made its way into the mainstream media. To wit: Societies become more efficient and "green" as they get wealthier. Whenever gross domestic product per capita reaches 5000 US dollars, 1987-size, the environment starts getting cleaner.[2] The environment in the US began getting cleaner years before Richard Nixon invented the EPA.

Another trend, even more telling and less ballyhooed by the news networks, is that when populations gain wealth, their birth rates slow. The United Nations has quietly published its concerns that the real population problem 50 years from now will be under-replacement.[3] It seems the economic reasons people had for making lots of babies 100 years ago have disappeared, and people are having children only as they want them. The free market solves its own problems, even the most dire ones feared by the population-bomb alarmists of the 1960s and '70s.

The market's decisions always precede government intervention in the market. The Securities Exchange Commission (SEC) and other government interventions in the stock market took root only in the 20th century, whereas the historical roots of the New York Stock Exchange predate the United States itself. There were plenty of roads before the government began exercising its "right" of eminent domain and building them for us (and making them available to anyone who wants to use them, including the 9/11 terrorists). And there were plenty of schools, doing spectacular work, before the government decided that it should manage education centrally and forcibly.

---

2. Research details available at http://www.ncseonline.org/NLE/CRSreports/ Economics/econ-3.cfm?&CFID=13789910&CFTOKEN=4586154, as of May 2004.

3. See, for example, this one of many UN documents discussing government responses to widespread population aging and decline, at http://www.un.org/esa/population/ publications/popdecline/Zoubanov.pdf. Accessed May, 2004.

Now, yet again, the market has found a new, more efficient way to get more money out of a cow for the producer, and more value for you and me. I can only imagine the government regulations that will arise on the heels of this new discovery: Regulations on how many pounds of a given-sized cow must be made into steaks; regulations on how much waste is allowed…heck, whatever a legislator's heart desires.

There's more that government hasn't done yet to the beef cattle industry, but could in the near future. "Certified Angus" beef is certified by a professional association that bases its certifications on the lineage of the cattle. Angus cattle are found wherever ranches are found. The Angus trademark is not a guarantee of perfection, and there are competing beef cattle lines. But the cattle's lineage is a prime niche for government certification, especially once DNA coding is second nature for geneticists.

Right now, according to a rancher of my acquaintance, beef cattle ranching remains among the least-regulated industries. Give it a few decades. The lure of government largesse will have state and national legislators handing out more protections for American beef against, e.g., Brazilian and Argentinean beef, resulting only in higher prices and less variety for us; genetic, procedural, and other regulations (to protect existing ranchers against new competition from within the US); and anything else you can imagine. The result will be the same as it has been with sugar, potatoes, and plums: less variety, lower quality, less availability, and higher prices at retail.

It's funny how the occasional small, random news item can evoke a flood of sometimes little-known but important truisms about free markets and free people. None of us has the imagination to predict either how the market can suddenly make life better, more interesting and enjoyable, and less expensive; or how legislators and judges can find a new way to take consumer dreams and turn them into bland, overpriced realities. Let's hope the legislators don't discover beef cattle before we all have at least one chance to enjoy these new steaks.

LIBERTY IS HARD WORK

I wrote earlier that vegetable gardening is a small but satisfying and symbolic way to get the government—with its taxes on land, materials, shipping, labor, and sales, and its incessant and costly yet ineffective inspections and regulations—out of your food. I put my money where my pen was and grew vegetables myself. This allowed me to prove my point about the economic and gustatory efficiency of vegetable gardening, and even about the effectiveness of voluntary associations in production.

A nearby landowner agreed to let me use a small plot of land. Together we planted tomatoes, zucchini, okra, jalapenos, and herbs, all of which did well; and strawberries, carrots, and cantaloupes that didn't do well. The minutiae I learned from the experience, and still remember, include: It is easy to water a garden too much; it is difficult to keep out grass and weeds; birds are a costly nuisance; some herbs are finicky about everything; there are 50 ways to mess up soil (and 100 ways to get it right); and so on. Mostly, I learned that gardening successfully is hard work, oregano is impossible to kill, basil can grow into a bush three feet in height and diameter, and voluntary associations can work quite nicely.

The "work" part is the catch. Labor is naturally aversive to all creatures; so much so, and so naturally so, that none of us gives the slightest indication otherwise. That workaholic you know who finished a PhD at age 24 and had tenure by age 29, convincing everyone that hard work made him happy: Ask him why he doesn't store all his books on the highest possible shelves, at the other end of the house from where he uses them. The college football coach who works 100-hour weeks during the playing season keeps his pens and pencils in the center desk drawer, not on top of the filing cabinet.

When reduced to these terms, the universal disutility of labor is seen not to be a matter of laziness, but a matter of efficiency. There are some things we want, such as a high income, a certain college degree, or career milestones for which we will work hard; but along that road we save labor wherever possible. We even find the most efficient study methods in earning that coveted degree. The trick is recognizing when hard work will bring a great payoff. This is the case with liberty.

Which brings me to the evangelist Billy Graham. In a recent newspaper column (brought to my attention—in this context, no less—by my landlord), a reader asked Rev. Graham how to change the mind of an atheist family member. Graham replied that persuasion might be ineffective because many atheists secretly suspect there is truth in Christianity, but they refuse to make a move because it would mean changing their priorities, lifestyles, and worst of all, thinking. That would be hard work. This is a good place to quote Bertrand Russell: "Most people would sooner die than think. In fact, they do."

In the same vein, libertarian radio personality Neal Boortz is fond of using the word "sheeple" to describe Americans who see nothing wrong with Social Security, Medicare, Medicaid, the Department of Energy, the EPA, the Department of Education, and other government departments and entitlement programs. Put another way, sheeple don't see enough wrong with such things to spur them to action. They would rather be led than lead. Much of our populace can be described by the term "sheeple," given the outcome of our 2002 presidential election—a dead heat between Al Gore, an obvious lover of socialist entitlement programs and tax increases for "the rich" (read, the ones who make life better for the rest of us); and George W. Bush, whose handlers coined the term "compassionate conservatism" to show his own fondness for socialist entitlement programs and expansive government.

Even the founding fathers recognized the disutility of labor (as Economics 101 textbooks refer to it today) in the Declaration of Independence. From the second paragraph of the Declaration: "Prudence, indeed, will dictate that Governments long established should not be changed for light and transient causes; and accordingly all experience hath shewn, that mankind are more disposed to suffer, while evils are sufferable, than to right themselves by abolishing the forms to which they are accustomed."

And what are the disincentives to liberty? You'd have to plan for your own retirement, if you wish to have one (the very notion of retirement was invented by our federal government[4]); you'd have to buy your own flood insurance if you insist on living on a flood plain; you'd have to read and understand many other insurance policies, including medical, homeowner's, etc. very carefully, because your selection of providers would have a substantial impact on your well being in an emergency and there'd be no government bailout for you.

You'd have to take a more active, participatory role in community governance (for example, the federal government wouldn't be in charge of your local blood-alcohol limit for driving on public roads, nor for safety standards in your work-place and grocery store); you'd have to buy a gun, learn how to use it, and take responsibility for teaching your children not to do stupid things with it; and the list goes on and on. Of course, freedom-loving people who act in their own enlightened self-interest do all these things already.

But it's easier to vote for whoever promises you the most handouts, and to let him take the money for those handouts from someone else, such as the person who runs the business that employs you. Liberty means that in a strong sense, you become the person who runs the business that employs you. And it is always the case, but particularly right now, that to promote liberty you would have to speak out in opposition to anything a government does that threatens to take it away.

---

4. Read *The Revolution of 1935: The Secret History of Social Security*, by Gregory Bresiger, for free online at http://www.mises.org/journals/essays/bresiger.pdf.

Thus, in addition to having to work harder, you'd occasionally have to risk being unpopular, at least among those who enjoy the handouts, or worse, who derive much of their self-esteem from nationalist sentiment and identify themselves with their government. If liberty requires saying something politically incorrect, it means stepping out on a limb.

There are other reasons liberty hasn't caught on in the United States, not the least of which is public education that stresses loyalty to the federal government (but not so much to state or city governments) and the virtue of nationalism over federalism. That same public education system completely omits significant historical facts and issues that underscore the wealth and security that arise under liberty as against the hardship and misery that correlate perfectly with increasing government control of people's lives.

Why were we ready for liberty in the 1770s? The founders were educated and courageous. While none of them had a government-approved education, the founders studied and understood history and philosophy far better than most of us do today. That gave them a good basis for understanding where their government had gone wrong (read the Declaration of Independence for the government abuses they endured and enumerated).

Alexander Hamilton could name the ancient Greek city-states and their forms of democratic government, and the results these forms brought.[5] Thomas Jefferson, when writing letters to friends, occasionally wrote in Greek or Latin to make a point, showing not only his erudition but also what he expected of his correspondents.[6] Because of their education, the founders knew when government was overstepping its proper bounds; and possibly because of their upbringing (the nuclear family, mostly Christian), they were willing to risk life and limb to set things right.

Most Americans today haven't read the Constitution that binds them; indeed, most federal government employees couldn't tell you much about it. Lovers of liberty have the daunting task of educating themselves and their brethren, and mustering the discipline and courage to live by their principles. It's hard work. Positions are available now. All it takes to get started is a small plot and a few seeds.

---

5.   See *The Federalist Papers*, available online on many websites.
6.   Available on many websites also, though this site is particularly well organized: http://odur.let.rug.nl/~usa/P/tj3/writings/brf/jeflxx.htm, accessed May 2004.

5

Italian Food

Italian food is the best cuisine in the world. The variety and freshness of ingredients, the combinations and recipes, the histories and stories, and the unbridled, un-self-conscious passion with which Italians approach food and eating help explain the superiority of their cuisine. The food is even more amazing considering the political circumstances under which the cuisine has developed, as I'll discuss more below. The Italians have been far more oppressed than the Swiss (who have no distinct national cuisine of their own) and even the English and Irish (whose national cuisines are weapons of mass destruction). And no, the political oppression and silliness to which the Italians have been subjected aren't responsible, either—note that no one extols the wonders of Russian or Cambodian cooking. If I had to eat exclusively of one national cuisine every meal for the rest of my life, it would be Italian.

BALSAMIC VINEGAR AND PARMESAN CHEESE

If you lock a hamster in an exercise wheel and make the wheel turn for days on end, the hamster will learn to take micro-naps of a second or less in duration. This way, the hamster stays alive, and borderline sane, until the wheel stops. (I don't remember what ridiculous academic researcher went to the trouble, and harassed the hamsters, to learn this, but my writing about it probably represents the first time the knowledge gained has been used in any productive way.) The lesson: Critters adapt.

I'm not an expert on Italian political history, but have scanned the perhaps 150,000 words devoted to it by *Encyclopedia Britannica* (heck, *Huckleberry Finn* was only 110,000 words). To make it brief, it's fair to say that since 320 A.D., any given region of Italy has seen its government change an average of once per generation (sometimes once every few years); has seen everything from Catholic to communist to anarcho-family rule; and has been governed by French, German,

Spanish, Greek, and/or other interlopers. And yet, Italian food is the most long-storied, developed, sophisticated, and sublime cuisine mankind has had the pleasure of sampling. The lesson: People do more than adapt. Two food items, balsamic vinegar and Parmesan cheese, make the point.

Balsamic vinegar, that black stuff, has been around for over a millennium. White grapes (yes, white) have been grown in and around the city of Modena, on the same hills, all this time. The grapes are mashed into a big pot and boiled until the volume in the pot is reduced by half or more. The remaining liquid, the "must," is poured into wooden barrels.

Each family keeps a room full of these barrels—sometimes 20 rows, 20 or more barrels per row. When the vinegar is 20 years old, it's poured out of the last row of barrels into bottles for sale. The vinegar in the penultimate row of barrels is then poured into the last row, and so on, until the stuff most recently boiled is poured into the first set of barrels. It takes 20 years for the best stuff to get to market.

The barrels are old. Each row may be of a different wood from the next. When a given barrel gets so old and saturated that it begins to leak—the vinegar is seeping through the actual wood, not the cracks between the staves—they'll build a new barrel tightly around the old one so they can keep using the same wood. I've seen a photo of a barrel in use today that was built in the 1300s.

The 20-year-old vinegar is taken to a government consortium for tasting and grading. It is given a rating, and the highest rating means the vinegar can sell for $30 an ounce (that small bottle you get in the grocery store, if it were the good stuff, would be $200). The consortium tasters must train through a 9-year apprenticeship. If your vinegar doesn't make the top grade, you may age it a few more years and bring it back to the consortium for another tasting, or sell it for less than it would get if it had the consortium's stamp of highest approval. I've seen a film clip of one of these vinegar judges at work, tasting and writing notes and tasting again. They take their jobs and themselves seriously.

The Modena families who make this vinegar didn't even think of marketing it until the early 20th century. It was for family use, and was given as a gift to friends and visiting dignitaries. It has a sweet, pungent flavor. You don't need to spend $30 an ounce to get an idea; get one of those 6-ounce, $4 bottles at your local grocery. Pour some into a saucer, and dip your garlic bread into it. Trust me. Or soak parmesan cheese in it. Use it in oil-and-vinegar salad dressings. When the rank-and-file Italians buy a bottle of the really good stuff, they bring it to restaurants with them, along with an eyedropper to apply it to the food.

Parmesan cheese is made in Parma. The families and companies that make it have been using the same breed of red cattle (for its flavorful milk) fed on the same diet (grasses grown on the same hillsides) for over 400 years. The apprenticeship to become a cheese maker takes 12 years. The town has a school for it. Italian Parmesan is, in the minds of some chefs, the king of cheeses. The chefs who believe this are probably correct.

The cheese, formed into wheels (85-pound wheels, $1600 each to you and me), is stored in a warehouse for aging for 26 months. The old government man who tends the warehouse hits each wheel with a small mallet, listening for imperfections. If he hears any, the cheese is marked as a factory second, and is sold only within the local region.[1] This man can dig a sample out of a random wheel, and by sniffing and tasting, tell you how many months it's been in the warehouse—even though there are different families making this cheese. The government's involved in one more step, by the way: It is required by law that the leftovers from making the Parmesan cheese are used to make ricotta cheese.[2]

An Italian never knows what to expect from his government. That's not to say Italians aren't passionate about it; many have died over the last two millennia to make Italy a just nation (the definitions of "just" covering the entire political spectrum), and they've been experimenting with strong federalism/weak nationalism (upon which notion the US was united under our Constitution, if you read *The Federalist Papers*) in recent decades. But then again, they're passionate about everything, from opera to espresso.

Their food is evidence they're doing more than taking micro-naps. In fact, the unbelievable development of their culinary artistry teaches more lessons than can be absorbed. For example, like the Amish, they ignore the government as much as possible and create wonderful lives in their own neighborhoods. Unlike the

1. The people of Parma have learned what smugglers learned during prohibition in the US. When exporting, transportation adds costs. If you, the customer, are going to pay $5 more to get a product from farther away, are you more willing to add $5 to a $5 product, or to a $50 product? Clearly, the better goods are more marketable in export than the worse ones. The risk premium charged by smugglers during prohibition added (say) the same $5 to each bottle, so lo and behold, the more expensive foreign boozes sold better during prohibition than did the cheaper ones.

2. The government in Parma has learned something about economies of scope (those circumstances where it's more efficient for a single firm to produce two items than for two firms to produce them separately). In the US, we see this where lumber companies also make oriented strand board, or when 3M makes both duct tape and masking tape. Our entrepreneurs discovered this without the aid of a taxpayer-funded consortium.

hamster, rather than merely surviving they lead the world in the most glorious and sinless of sensual pleasures. They make the rest of us want to be lustier, heartier, and happier, in spite of the administrative squalor in which they have dwelt in perpetuity. While the government has changed many times, the cheese and vinegar reached their peaks of refinement centuries ago and have only improved since—if they've changed at all.

But what if the government weren't involved in so many of their affairs? (For example, their tax rates are actually higher than ours.) What if they had political stability, or even the absence of politics, in which to develop their culture? For a taste of where the imagination might go, consider how many Beethovens or Newtons we might have seen come from Africa and South America by now if governments on those continents were more concerned with allowing unfettered economic development than with consolidating their powers over the corpses of their rivals. As for an Italian example, what varieties of sweet, pungent vinegars might there be if the people of Modena didn't have a government consortium telling them how their vinegar should taste?

People—individuals, families, entrepreneurs, communities—doing their own thing are the ultimate source of anything good. By contrast, governments, however brilliant their conception, historically always grow to the point where they do little more than retard our economic and cultural development.

COOK ITALIAN OR DIE

Die unfulfilled, that is. However many umpteen distinct national cuisines exist, with many having umpteen of their own regional cuisines (does anybody confuse Texas cooking with Louisiana?), Italian remains Number One. Just as an aside, doctors at the Harvard School of Health have decided that the typical Italian diet—including the red wine and olive oil, though excluding some of the pasta—is a better bet for health and longevity than the 1992 Government Food Pyramid, obedience to which could do nothing but fatten you.[3]

Italians (I lived in Italy as a child) are friendly and open, and there is as much variety from the heel to the top of the boot as there is in any country—southern Italy is as different from northern as Yankee pot roast is from southern barbecue. There is virtually no ingredient or classical style that doesn't find a home somewhere in Italy. And you don't have to be a chef: Tour any of the foodwhatever.com

---

3.   See the write-up by physicians at http://www.lewrockwell.com/miller/miller10.html.

sites, and many of the best Italian dishes are well within reach of even the kitchen novice.

To give you an idea of how good, and how easy, Italian cooking can be, I include the following—a menu I made for family one summer, in celebration of Friday. The dishes are all my own, but are an example of what can be developed with inspiration from Italian cooking. This is all easy stuff:

Antipasto—chunks of Canadian bacon, Havarti cheese, calamata olives, and marinated artichoke hearts, all spread on a little plate; on the side, a dip of (store-bought) Italian salad dressing with some balsamic vinegar mixed in.

Pasta—olive oil, chopped black olives, black pepper, and diced bacon, sautéed. Some hot red pepper flakes, if you like. Cooked spiral pasta stirred in, and parmesan cheese grated over the top just prior to serving.

Postpasto (my own term, for an additional appetizer course after the pasta)—white grapes, sliced in half, marinated overnight in white wine and white vinegar. Prior to serving, sprinkle with black pepper and walnut bits and chunks of Gruyere cheese. Without the walnut bits and cheese, this would be the Fettuccine Alfredo garnish mentioned earlier.

Entrée—this is a little more time-consuming. Veal scaloppini, seared in clarified butter and olive oil (always extra-virgin), then set aside. Diced white onion, bell pepper, jalapeño, and carrot, sautéed in clarified butter and olive oil with black pepper, then diced garlic added. Deglaze with red wine and beef stock, add diced/seeded/peeled Roma tomatoes. Add the veal, simmer and stir for 45 minutes or so to thoroughly tenderize the veal, thicken the sauce, and blend the flavors. Add tomato paste, if needed, to thicken; add wine or stock occasionally if the liquid reduces too much. On presentation, sprinkle liberally with fresh basil. On the side: big slices of Italian bread, coated with butter, olive oil, and fresh mashed garlic, sautéed briefly each side, then cover with sliced eggplant, black pepper, and shredded Romano cheese. Pass under the broiler to melt the cheese a little.

Salad—a pre-mix of different lettuces, with a raspberry vinaigrette dressing. On the side: slices of Roma tomato with one big basil leaf on each one. Grate Romano cheese over the top of the whole thing, but another good and simple salad would be tomato slices with fresh (from the deli) Mozzarella cheese, basil leaves, balsamic vinegar, and olive oil.

Dessert: something I got out of a box. I don't know much about desserts, even though I'm perfectly happy to eat them.

If you study the tiniest bit of Italian cooking, a feast is well within your grasp. My example isn't extraordinary by Italian standards, either. At an Italian wedding in 1969, my parents counted at least eight courses, each one delicious, and I've heard of celebration feasts that take all day. Again, "simple" and "gourmet" are adjectives that go together in Italy. Pasta sauces can work with three ingredients (e.g., olive oil, red pepper flakes, and bacon; butter, cream, and white wine), and entrees can be complete with maybe four (e.g., veal chops seared in olive oil, sprinkled liberally with grated parmesan cheese, and a paper-thin slice of prosciutto over the top).

Be sure to have plenty of a good Italian dry red wine and cool water to drink.

Spread the word. Increase demand for Italian cooking where you live. It'll improve our lifestyles and our health.

Eat Italian and Live!

I might as well talk about what I actually eat on a daily basis. I live on a facsimile of the Mediterranean diet developed by Harvard researchers and explained by LewRockwell.com's Dr. and Mrs. Miller.[4] The differences between the Mediterranean diet and our government's hog-fattening diet for people are that the Mediterranean diet's recommendations are lower on red meats, butter, and white flour; and higher on plant oils and (insistence on) whole grains than the government plan. I differ from the Mediterranean diet's recommendations by eating a bit more red meat and eggs, less grains in general—and then only whole grains, usually in the form of 100% whole-wheat pasta or bread—and virtually no legumes, as a matter of convenience.

This diet is relatively convenient and affordable; and I stick with it because I'd be happy to live on nothing but Italian food. To give you an idea how good-eats this diet can be, here's a typical day for me:

Breakfast: Bacon and eggs; whole-wheat toast with olive oil, garlic, and Parmesan cheese; a sliced tomato with olive oil, balsamic vinegar, and Parmesan cheese; coffee and water (both from a 79-cent gallon of distilled water); and plenty of salt and black pepper. During the day, at my desk I'll have some raw carrots, grapes, an apple, and mixed nuts. For dinner: A small serving of whole-wheat pasta, coated after cooking with olive oil, garlic, and parmesan cheese; a piece of tilapia cooked in olive oil; some raw baby spinach with olive oil, balsamic

---

4.   ibid.

vinegar, and parmesan cheese. At bedtime: 5 or 10 Jelly Bellies and a shot of Kentucky bourbon. When I stick with this diet for even a few days in a row, I lose weight. I usually stick with it Monday through Friday.

One recommendation about the salt: The regular stuff at the store has iodine and some anti-caking agents. Most serious cooks gave it up long ago for sea salt and kosher salt, both of which are probably better for you than the regular stuff. Note, however, that while kosher salt is used by all the famous chefs now and is the most-often recommended for serious cooking, it still has anti-caking agents. Instead, look for canning and pickling salt, which is the only one that's 100% pure NaCl, made that way so it doesn't produce any colored deposits in your preserves. Canning and pickling salt is also far less expensive than kosher salt and sea salt.

I realize all that olive oil, Parmesan cheese, and balsamic vinegar might sound monotonous day after day. I do take a break on weekends, sometimes going to an Italian restaurant or a barbecue joint, but you can put on fat quickly eating all the simple carbohydrates you'll get eating out. And a good extra-virgin olive oil, and good, whole Parmesan—even from Wisconsin, particularly since it's 1/3 the price of the Italian (real) stuff—won't tire your taste buds quickly. They're too good.

Now, about the olive oil: There are at least dozens of brand names, and within each brand there are at least two varieties. The varieties include extra virgin, virgin, pure, mild, light, extra light, and a few others. "Extra virgin, first cold pressed," is the only one you want if you're going to go to the expense of using olive oil at all. "Virgin" means first pressing—the oil collected from the first pressing of a batch of olives. The leftover olive mash is combined with other leftover batches of olive mash to make subsequent batches of oil, which might be called "pure," "light," or something else. "First" is redundant to "virgin," but "cold pressed" carries the additional information that the olives were crushed without the presence of heat, which is a good thing. "Extra" means it's the best this particular producer has to offer in terms of taste, color, and aroma. Anything other than extra-virgin, first-cold-pressed will be higher in acidity, and lower in fruity olive flavor and aroma.

So if you didn't already, you know now that you should look for "extra virgin, first cold pressed." The lighter (more highly refined/processed) olive oils are better for highest-heat frying and baking, and have little or no olive flavor. Hence, save your money and buy oils made from other plants—corn, peanut—for deep frying and baking, and get only the best-flavored olive oil for daily use with salads, bread, pasta, and sautéing. One interesting trick Graham Kerr devised is to mix extra-light olive oil with 1/16 part toasted sesame seed oil. This produces a smoky, buttery aroma. It's not worth the trouble, though, if you can have the extra-virgin stuff mixed with a little clarified butter and you don't have a cholesterol problem.

There is an entire industry devoted to critical discussion of the merits and demerits of particular brands of extra-virgin, first-cold-pressed olive oil. This much they get right: Read the labels. If it says made in Italy, keep looking on the label for whether the olives came from Italy; they might have been grown over a landfill in Slobovia. Otherwise, the differences between one brand and another are often a matter of who had the best crop last year. You can spend $20 and more for a 12-ounce bottle of the Italian stuff, but if you're going to use it at the rate I do, go for the Spanish stuff: $7.59 for 32 ounces (I use about 8 ounces a week for myself, though some of that ends up in the bottoms of pans and bowls). Whatever smells and tastes good to you is gourmet.

Like Irish and German folk tunes and classic literary conflicts, anything that makes it through several hundred, or thousand, years of continuous human use must be good. Oil has been pressed from olives for at least 4400 years. Other food items with long histories—wine, beer, roasted animal flesh, salt, spices, raw vegetables—tell the same story: When billions of food lovers, living and dead, agree on something for many centuries, they're likely to be right.

A diet full of olive oil, garlic, and parmesan cheese is luxurious. That it keeps you healthy, doesn't make you fat, and doesn't involve much work seems too good to be true. Then again, that's how I feel about all Italian food.

BACHELOR CHOW

The glories of the Mediterranean diet notwithstanding, eating healthfully (raw veggies and a few fruits, fresh meat and fish, that sort of thing) takes a lot of time and energy. I'm probably at the grocery store four times a week, and in the kitchen cooking every weekday evening and morning. A good diet can require a lot of appliances, too, if you're not resourceful. So we bachelors (I consider myself a Southern Oscar Madison) have been known to find shortcuts. Fortunately, in spite of my bad housekeeping, I haven't descended to the point of using underwear as a coffee filter. I'm told it works pretty well. Here are a couple of shortcuts I've developed that I think are decent enough to publicize:

Coffee

Don't spend big money on the Starbucks-type faddy stuff. Unless you're a rabid connoisseur, and insist on beans from a certain region, go for the cheaper stuff. Refrigerate or freeze after opening. To avoid buying any kind of coffee machine, I bought one nice brass dishwasher-safe coffee filter. I put a cup's worth of distilled water into a pan, and bring it to a boil. Then I take the pan off the heat, let it cool for a few seconds, measure the ground coffee straight into the pan, and stir a bit to get it all submerged. After letting it soak for 2–3 minutes, I pour it straight into a cup, through the filter. Finer grinds of coffee (I grind mine finely, to get more flavor) result in some sediment getting through the filter, but that'll sink to the bottom of the mug. What you get is a BIG coffee flavor and aroma—fully as good as what you smell when you first open a new package—without any bitterness.

There is some disagreement about espresso. Some say a really dark roast is the wrong way to go about it—that a medium or light roast, subjected to the right pressure, concentration, and temperature, will give the best results. I just happen to like the dark stuff I bought; I make no claim to being right about it. Also, without the pressure, it's doubtful I get as strong a brew as a machine would produce. I can just about float a horseshoe on mine, so I'm not worried about it. (It's still not bitter.)

There's also dispute over whether distilled water is the best choice for coffee brewing. Bottled water of other kinds, such as spring water or that Coca-Cola Company stuff with trace minerals added, reportedly gives the coffee more sorts of molecules onto which to attach its flavor. My coffee doesn't lack for flavor, though. And I'll take my 79-cent-per-gallon distilled stuff, which is as pure as you can buy anyway, over the $3/gallon stuff in the half-liter bottles. Plus, when I get to the point of using underwear as a filter, the distilled water won't make any mineral stains.[5]

Olive Spread

I make several days' worth of this at a time, and put it on toast and pasta. It's a classic spread, but doesn't get the fame it deserves. Dice a handful of green or black olives; add half that much (each) of diced nuts, garlic, and Parmesan cheese; add salt, pepper, and olive oil. Stir, mash, whatever; store in an airtight container in the fridge. I haven't tried using the food processor, as I prefer the

---

5.   I did hear from one reader, another coffee-loving bachelor, who thought it necessary to tell me to be sure to use clean underwear—as though he'd learned the hard way.

old-fashioned chef's knife way, but a food processor should work well. If the coffee doesn't wake you up, the green-olive spread on toast will. Try it as a salad dressing with some balsamic vinegar.

Nuts

Unless you have an allergy to them, nuts are good for you. You can save money by buying nuts in bulk, freezing some, and roasting a bunch as you need them. Just melt some whole, unsalted butter, with salt and cayenne pepper to taste. Put the buttered nuts in a single layer in a dish, and microwave them for about 3 minutes. Alternately, you can roast them for 10 minutes at 350 degrees F, or all day at 200 degrees. Store them in the fridge. I'm partial to pecans (pronounced "PUCKons") and walnuts, but that may be because they're the cheapest in bulk right now.

Some of my shortcuts might be more offensive than others to dilettantes. For example, I use a good Wisconsin imitation of parmesan cheese (but not the powdered stuff in the green shaker). It comes already grated. I've compared it side-by-side with the real imported cheese from Parma, and the difference is trivial. If anything, the Wisconsin is nuttier and more intensely flavorful, while the stuff from Parma can be powdery. Whatever government subsidies they may or may not get, our folks in Wisconsin still have to compete with the famous European cheeses with regard to taste, and they do an excellent job.

If you have any good shortcuts of your own, I'd be glad to hear them. The only thing better than eating tons of healthy, rich, Italianate food every day is doing it without much effort. *That* is wealth.

HOW TO GET STARTED

Cooking is not necessarily isomorphic with culture. Italians once were so cultured that J. S. Bach himself composed often "in the Italian style," Italian opera was the center of the musical universe, and Italian painters and scientists were at the forefront of human artisanship and technology. Alas, much of that high culture faded away before Italian cooking became everything it is. The tomato, after all, didn't find its way into Italian recipes much before the 19th century, since the tomato was not widespread in Europe much before then.

But you already know that the roots of Italian culinary supremacy reach back 500 years, to the beginnings of Parmesan cheese; and another 500 years, to the beginnings of balsamic vinegar; and probably another 1000 years before that, if you read up on the daily lives of the wealthier citizens of ancient Rome.

But I digress. My real point here is that if you study enough Italian cooking, you'll see that it's easy to think in its terms. You can take your own homegrown recipes and make them Italian. You will likely improve them, but even if you don't, you'll still create gustatory memories—the stuff of roses in December.

My walnut chili, described earlier, calls for good tender beef, simmered in beef stock until it falls apart, with apples, thyme, walnuts, onions, and jalapenos. If you haven't tried it, you don't know what you're missing, and you don't know how sweet and savory flavors can combine to your delight (even if you've already enjoyed Chinese sweet-and-sour pork). To make it Italian, the recipe can be modified this way: Beef and veal; beef stock; onions; pine nuts; basil and flat-leaf parsley; red pepper flakes; and oranges.

There's nothing you can cook that can't be Italianized. Another of my better dishes is vegetable pie. I sauté onions, potatoes, carrots, bell peppers, asparagus or broccoli, and add some parsley and tons of cheddar cheese; put all this in a pie crust, and bake. It seems too simple to be as good as it is, but food excellence is not synonymous with complexity.

To Italianize the pie, make it with black olives, mushrooms, red and Vidalia onions (yes, Vidalias are from Georgia; to quote Ring Lardner, "shut up he explained"), parsley and basil, fresh baby spinach, red bell pepper, and Parmesan cheese. Sauté most of that (except the spinach and cheese) in butter and extra-virgin olive oil, sprinkle on some red pepper flakes, and bake the whole pile in one of those frozen pie crusts. Put a crust over the top. A little egg wash or some butter on top of the crust, and you get that shiny brown look that impresses guests.

There doesn't really have to be a non-food-related point to every food you can mention. The enjoyment of spectacular food, or just really good food in large quantities (southern barbeque is a case in point), is an end in itself. There needn't be a political or moral implication, or a practical application, to appreciate and simply enjoy such human artifices as the paintings and sculptures of da Vinci and Michelangelo; Texas-style smoked beef brisket; or Newton's calculus.

That such efforts have, in one way or another, served to accelerate mankind's progress is icing on the cake. Indeed, such efforts do more than serve as paving bricks in the road to progress. They illuminate our forward progression, guiding our future efforts. Through all their political struggles, Italian ingredients and recipes have motored forward, unstoppably, and resulted in a cuisine that celebrates freshness, creativity, variety, purity, beauty, and a love of cooking and eating, of all of which the world properly ought to be jealous.

What to do with this knowledge? Practically, you should study Italian cooking, and learn to combine relatively common ingredients in new and delectable ways. Celebrate God's bounty and enjoy it without guilt (but get some exercise). Strategically, take a lesson from the Italians: Understand politics, and anything else outside of voluntary, peaceful behavior, for what it is—a stumbling block in mankind's progress toward a peaceful, stable, and delightfully edible future.

6

Southern Food

The US is divided into distinct food regions. The Northeast and East Coast have their seafood and Yankee pot roast; California has that Frenchified Left Coast flavor, with the avocado pizzas and cinnamon latte; the Southwest exploits fresh peppers, corn, beans, and cactus; and the South has its own cuisine, known by many names: soul food, down-home cooking, white trash cooking, whatever. Louisiana, of course, is a region unto itself, combining local and Southern flavors with stylistic roots coming from France and Africa.

Southern food, like all others (except that of the British Isles), is worth exploring in its own right. Southerners love freedom, women, meat, and strong flavors, and as a result, we've developed a cuisine unique to our region and traditions.

WHAT'S SO SPECIAL ABOUT SOUTHERN FOOD?

Visiting the grocery stores and flipping past the Food Network on July 4, I was reminded that all the great barbeque traditions are southern. Even restaurants in Yankee country, such as Red Bones in Somerville, Massachusetts, advertise their barbeque as southern-style. I'm sure the whole country has heard of Memphis and Texas barbeque; St. Louis is famous for it, too. In other Southeastern states, residents don't as often trust the tradition to restaurants, which is why you haven't heard of "Alabama barbecue" or "Georgia barbecue" though it's as good in those places as anywhere. Why is great barbecue so inextricably linked with the south? Here are some ideas:

First, the weather. Southerners are swathed in weather that lets them cook outdoors most of the year. After a few hundred years of that, traditions develop—look at Italy, just over twice the size of Georgia and yet endowed with several spiritedly competitive "regional" cuisines, each claiming its soil and weather are better than everyone else's.

Then there's hunting. The quintessential southern vee-hickle is the four-wheel-drive pickup truck with a toolbox and gun rack. Southerners love to hunt deer, but they'll hunt almost anything. I say "they" rather than "we" because, though a southerner, I'm not a hunter. I've done the killing-, cleaning-, and eating-a-quadruped thing, and while it's satisfying enough, it can get to be a chore.[1] That's what ranchers and grocers are for.

But there are those who don't tire of hunting, for reasons that go beyond weather and sport. Aside from the fact that it reacquaints you with the life cycle, food chain, and raw nature, hunting is an escape from the food-nannying government. By taking the effort (and skill) to locate a delicious wild animal, and kill and butcher and cook and serve it yourself, you remove the state from various aspects of the transaction, such as government inspectors deciding whether the meat passes code (and adding their costs to it, with government "guarantees" that it's safe), government adding costs at various levels to your purchase of it from the grocery store, and so on.

As an exercise in personal liberty, hunting is a rare holdover from an era when Washington, D.C. didn't impose itself into your diet. And the South is the area in the nation where resides the greatest broad base of people who still love liberty and will work to enjoy it. Note, alas, the government still gets involved as much as possible by requiring hunting licenses—their final edict to the effect that you can't be allowed to eat without government approval.

Even meat itself, and the act of barbecuing, are manly things, therefore suited to the Southern personality. There's fire, there's blood, there are strong spices and beer, and often there are vivacious women nearby, ready to enjoy the feast.

Hence the North, particularly the urban Northeast, just doesn't revel in barbecue in the same way we do in the south. Perhaps this is partly because northeast-urban public schools have been fighting to remove manliness from the behavior of boys for long enough that Time magazine ran a cover story a few years back in which they acted astounded to learn that men and women are different at all.

Fear not, northern brethren: Meat is good for you—it builds strong muscles (assuming you exercise) and healthy red blood. So you don't even have to be manly to love meat; just smart. Pork is the other white meat. Beef is what's for dinner. And tofu, sprouts, and those meat-free burger-like food product things just aren't the same on the grill.

---

1.   But see Humberto Fontova's book, *The Hellpig Hunt* (available at Amazon.com), to learn how much fun hunting can be, and why.

So take a chance: Procure your own living food, even if it means fishing or buying a live lobster at the grocer's, and get back to nature and in touch with a little piece of the liberty we once had. It does wonders for the blood.

Now you know a big part of what makes Southern food so special: It's produced by Southerners.

SOUTHERN BARBECUE

As long as I'm on the topic of southern cuisine, I might as well talk about the actual food in some detail. And it doesn't make sense to talk about southern food unless you begin with barbecue.

The origins of the term "barbecue" and the cooking methods associated with it are lost to history. The term itself may derive from a French term meaning something to the effect of "head to tail," and today, barbecue often involves cooking the entire animal. Some stories say the tradition in the US dates to the 1700s in Virginia and North Carolina, among colonists who may have learned the technique from American Indians or Caribbean aborigines. Given that the basic requisites are meat and fire, barbecuing probably dates back about as far as the human use of fire.

As to the term "barbecue" today, different people take it different ways. There is "grilling," in which the meat is within several inches of the flames, such as with an hibachi, and you get grill marks. This method is also known as "direct cooking," or cooking with direct heat. Then there's "smoking," where the meat is nowhere near the flames, and the hot smoke itself cooks the meat. According to 19th-century cowboy traditions, the meat should be cooked at around 200 degrees F., so any place near a flame would be too hot. In my water smoker, I shoot for 210 degrees, but anywhere between 190 and 220 is usually okay. The smoke flavor itself is part of the objective; keeping the meat tender and juicy is the rest (though it can take real mastery to produce a tender, juicy barbecued brisket).

So for "barbecue," some people think smoking and some think grilling. It would be helpful if we could come up with some additional terms—one for smoking and then slathering with barbecue sauce, one for smoking while basting with barbecue sauce, another for grilling while basting. Perhaps another term for grilling and then slathering would be useful; then yet another for smoking and then not using any sauce.

For now, when somebody sells or otherwise offers you something they claim has been barbecued, look around or ask how it was cooked. You're not being rude; cooking meat is an art, and the more you can learn about the flavors and textures that result from different techniques, the better. Most cooks and chefs are pleased to hear "how did you do this?"

At cook-offs, Texans often will smoke a piece of meat for ten hours or more, up to six feet away from the flame. A more common technique is to have the meat directly over the flame, but a low flame, with the whole contraption enclosed to keep the smoke inside. This is a more practical alternative to fabricating a grill that measures 3 by 5 by 7 feet.

There's pretty much one real regional difference in the South with regard to the meat. The vast majority of Dixie, upon hearing "barbecue," assumes pork. Texans don't. Texans generally assume beef brisket. As to the wood used for smoking, there is disagreement, but the differences are found in every town and don't follow regional lines (except that some hardwoods were more available in some places than others in the past; today, you can get anything at a big grocery store).

Hickory and mesquite are the most popular smoking woods, though applewood and others are still seen here and there. The real disagreement is over whether the variety of wood matters much. There is virtually no disagreement that wood gives more smoke flavor than charcoal. There can be no disagreement at all that gas grills don't impart any smoke flavor. When you try it yourself, be sure to use commercial charcoal; for the smoke, use hardwood chips or chunks that have been soaked in water. That makes them smoke without quite catching fire. Complete combustion, where the wood flames up, is what you don't want. That gives you soot.

There are also differences with regard to sauces. In Texas, barbecued meat is usually served with sauce on the side if there is any sauce at all. My favorite restaurant in College Station, Tom's (now out of business following the death of the original owner), for their Aggie Special served half a raw onion, a 4-oz. slice of cheddar cheese, a pickle, and 8 ounces of whatever meat you wanted, all on a piece of butcher paper. They gave you a knife (no fork) and a jar of their own barbeque sauce. The meat choices were pork tenderloin; beef that could pass for filet mignon; polish sausage; and I forget what else. Maybe chicken. The sauce I remember: Thick, fresh, and hot from the cooking pot, but with very little flavor beyond tomato—no pepper heat, no vinegar tang, no sweetness, no real spicy piquancy.

That's probably not typical of Texas barbecue sauces. A list of ingredients from one of the self-proclaimed "best" Texas barbecue sauces begins with "tomato concentrate, distilled vinegar, corn syrup, salt, spices...." That would be typical of barbecue sauces around the country. Most will have a tomato base, vinegar, sweetener, a little garlic and onion, and some heat. They sometimes have a puckering tang from prepared (powdered) mustard or turmeric; and some have a little citrus flavoring of some sort. Mustard-based sauces, which tend to be less sweet than the brown sauces, show up in many places.

Mustard- and tomato-based are the basic two, with the tomato-based sauce being the most popular. However, eastern North Carolina and Virginia have a tradition of their own: A watery, vinegar-based sauce with no tomato, sugar, or mustard flavor. I ordered a bottle and tried it, and can report that it is similar to any "Louisiana" hot sauce (the ingredients of which should always be only vinegar, peppers, and salt). The North Carolina sauce added some other spices that gave it an extremely dry, almost bitter flavor, similar to a Thai pepper sauce. The particular one I sampled has won awards in North Carolina, but I felt that the bitter, Thai-tasting spices made the sauce seem to want for some sweetness, which impression does not accompany the taste of a Louisiana hot sauce.

If you haven't had the chance to sample any local Southern barbeque sauces, despair not: The flavor that best captures the typical sauce can be had for 99 cents—just buy a bottle of Kraft barbeque sauce. That isn't shameful, either. Remember that Kraft hires food scientists to develop sauces for a living, and they measure proportions in parts per million. Kraft, by the way, sells about 50 varieties, and they're all inexpensive and good. Don't spend $4 on a bottle of barbecue sauce—heck, Kraft makes the more expensive "gourmet" Bullseye sauces. They're not any better than the 99-cent stuff.

Lest you hear from a puffed-shirt Southerner or Texan that he wouldn't touch the bottled stuff, be advised that most of the ones who say that have a bottle of it at home right now. I've lived in the South, from DC to Texas, so I know. Don't be persuaded that it would be easy for someone who makes his own sauce a few times a year to do a better job than a group of professionals who do it every day, 52 weeks per year, with sophisticated equipment, access to lots of taste testers, and access to hundreds of ingredients.

Most local Southern sauces taste similar to one Kraft variety or another. At one of the most famous barbecue chains in the Southeast, Dreamland (based in Tuscaloosa, Alabama), the sauce tastes exactly like the regular Kraft with a little water and heat added. That the good local sauces and Kraft sauces are similar means only that Southerners and food giants are arriving at a good basic flavor.

And some of Kraft's 50 relatively new varieties probably are themselves imitations of, or inspired by, various local twists on the basic theme; and some are actual recipes sent in by customers. The big food producers conduct plenty of market and field research.

Indeed, just as government interventions lag behind the market's identification of needs and their solutions (e.g., in the early 20th century, the government decided to write child-labor laws after the economy began to generate enough wealth that children weren't any longer being sent to factories by their parents, and after special-interest groups decided they were outraged by a practice that was already going away), big corporations often get "new" food-product ideas from foods people already have. The Oreo probably wasn't even an exception. They won't tell, though; I tried to get information out of Kraft about where the new barbecue sauce ideas come from, and they refused to answer.

So, "barbecue," whatever the term means, isn't a Southern invention; surely it's as old as the hills. All we Southerners did was perfect it. The reasons why would be pure speculation, but they probably begin with the reasons I mentioned earlier—our better climate, our love of hunting and fishing, our greater sociability, our slower-paced life, and our tasty pigs; and end with the only possible result of millions of people enjoying a craft that requires them to do all the work every time: Innovations happen randomly, frequently, sometimes serendipitously, but inevitably.

That's the way it works with anything people produce. People see where a thing (say, a washing machine) could be improved; they set about to improve it; then they see the results. If the results appear to constitute a real improvement, they subject the thing to the rigors of the free market. If the market likes the change, it survives; otherwise, it disappears. Our lives always get better in the long run. Nobody, except a collector or hobbyist, would want to buy a new car today that was designed 40 years ago, because today's cars are better.

Yes, there are old recipes we still enjoy, but remember we had centuries to improve those already. But the next time you get home with a major grocery-store purchase (or from a major shopping trip to the mall), count the number of items that would have existed in the form you bought them 25 years ago—and that includes fresh produce—and consider whether you'd rather do without the differences. Then count how many of the differences were invented or produced by government.

SOUTHERN COOKING

Hillbillies eat. So do rednecks, rubes, hicks, and plowboys. We have all of those people in Alabama, and we take more than our share of ribbing for it from Yankees and other ne'er-do-wells. Hillbilly food is interesting, delicious, nutritious, and worth a second look. And Southern food is fun. The whole point of food is fun. And since I'm a Southerner, I am allowed to poke fun at us.

Corn dogs are fun, good nutrition on a stick. (Okay, maybe not good nutrition.) You can microwave them. About half the calories come from fat, mostly from the vegetable oil in which the corn breading was fried, but some from the spare packing-house-floor pig parts they put in the dog itself. I recommend them with Kraft honey barbecue sauce with some Tabasco mixed in, but they're good with French's yellow mustard as well. Some tater tots on the side (Heinz makes a ketchup that has the Tabasco already mixed in), and there's good eating.

Fritos, on which we have been known to pile canned chili and cheese, get over half of their calories from fat. You can get them with barbecue flavor powder sprinkled on. Canadians probably put gravy on them, Belgians mayonnaise. They're kosher, by the way, according to the Frito-Lay website.

Honestly, we eat some of the same stuff Yankees and other ne'er-do-wells eat; just more of it. That's not all bad—when I look at an over-50 male who's underweight, I'm more easily convinced that he's sickly than healthy. And there are fat, uncultured Yankees, too. Go to any bargain department store to see some. The difference is that a Southern redneck will say "howdy" instead of "shut up" when his beer belly bumps you in the checkout line.

There are other things Southerners eat more of than Yankees. I see all sorts of frozen things even I wouldn't touch at the grocery store. They sell chitterlings, necks, hocks, feet, and other parts I'm less familiar with. (But be sure to buy a smoked ham hock sometime. Put it in a pressure cooker with lots of water [read the directions for the cooker], then use the water to cook the rice for a jambalaya. You can take the meat off the hock and use it in the jambalaya, too.)

And we must be the only people on the planet who'll take a steak, cover it with breading and deep fry it, and smother it with milk gravy. Just writing about it makes me hungry. Add Tabasco.

We consider Pop-Tarts a food group.

If you want people who generally speak perfectly and eat a well-balanced diet, you don't need to visit Southerners or Yankees anyway. And stay away from the left coast. The most cultured folk in the US are in the heartland. Two of my own grandparents, who grew up out in the sticks in eastern Kansas (born in the

1890s), are examples. My grandmother was able to read and write Greek and Latin, and my grandfather blended his own green tea from three different unblended teas he could find at any general store in eastern Kansas in the 1920s. My other grandparents grew up making their own wine from grapes they grew themselves.

Of course, that kind of sophistication is only partly a "heartland" thing. I have a 1960s cookbook with recipes for calf brains and sweetbreads (glands), among other things. Whether the disappearance of brains from American grocery stores means we're less cultured than we once were, or merely that we've narrowed our tastes to the "best" items, I don't know. I'll have to eat brains once to be sure.

But if you want free-thinking people who aren't impressed by Washington, DC, come to the south. And naturally, just like "sophistication" for New Yorkers and "corn fed" for Iowans, "free thinking" doesn't describe 100% of us. Some Southern states, after all, helped elect Bill Clinton twice. Yeehaa.

But back to Southern food: Go anywhere in Yankeeland where a restaurateur wants to make money selling fried chicken, and he calls it "Southern fried chicken." And while you've heard of Texas barbecue and Memphis barbecue, you'll never hear of Minneapolis or Massachusetts barbecue. Southern food is so good, the rest of the country imitates it. We do see some Yankee food down here, but it's pretty much just the canned clam chowder, which doesn't sell well anyway.

As usual, the lessons learned are numerous when first one practices to talk about food: Culture is where you find it; Yankees can be annoying; and good eats is good eats, regardless whether some effete snob slaved over it for two hours uttering foreign expletives. Okay, the annoying Yankees part wasn't really proven, but that point is generally understood anyway. If you're a Yankee reading this, you can consider yourself an exception on the grounds that you liked the general idea of this book.

If you haven't been lately, start eating some Southern food. (Um…be sure to get an annual physical. No reason.) To get something genuinely Southern, stay away from Atlanta and any big cities in Florida. Find a small town, or look around in your grocery store. Your health, mood, and personality will improve.

OKAY, ACTUAL SOUTHERN FOODS

The fun has now been poked. In all seriousness, we should prepare our food the way we like, and Southerners do that. Ben Franklin is reported to have said "eat to live, don't live to eat." I suppose technically he was correct, but as long as your doctor isn't getting really mad at you, you should learn some techniques from Southern cooks. Slather some comfort on that food and enjoy.

Louisianans love "mud bugs," a.k.a. crawdads or crawfish; and they are indeed bugs, just as lobsters are kissing cousins of cockroaches. The people in Louisiana will boil crawfish in a giant pot with crabs, potatoes, leeks, onions, jalapenos, and whatever else is in the kitchen that might work (indeed, legend has it that "jambalaya" loosely translated means "what's in the fridge?"), along with about a cup of ground spices and dried herbs. I've seen a vintage cooking show where the cook was struggling to get the lid on the pot against all the crawdads and crabs struggling to get out. This is proper—you want to know the seafood is fresh. Only in Louisiana is boiling a form of performance art.

Southern cooking is definitely not all hillbilly. Continuing with Louisiana, you will find that people on the street, especially in south Louisiana, understand the use of a mirepois—a mix of aromatic vegetables, sautéed. Aromatics include carrots, onions, leeks, garlic, shallots, peppers of all kinds, and more: vegetables, herbs, spices, etc. that stand up to a good sauté. The ingredients chosen always have some essential volatile oils that bring flavor and aroma to the party.

The classical European continental technique is to sauté (high heat) or sweat (low heat) some aromatics; deglaze the pan with wine, stock, broth, whatever; "mount" the sauce with butter or cream; strain (or not) and serve with the meat that is naturally the centerpiece of the meal. You want a mirepois. Indeed, most south Louisianans will know the difference between the Cajun mirepois (onion, bell pepper, celery) and the French (onion, carrot, celery). Fewer people know the Italian than should—onion, garlic, then whatever you want from among bell pepper, hot red pepper flakes, carrot…sometimes Italians use anchovies as an aromatic.

Louisianans are known for putting heat into most of their savory dishes. Easy dishes use Tabasco or powdered cayenne pepper. When cooking from scratch, diced hot peppers are added to the mirepois. Cajun cooking, it should be said, is not typical of most Southern food: The classical techniques and general style derive from French cooking, which seems to owe its best aspects to inheritances from Italy, dating back to the paleoculinary epoch. The deepest roots of Cajun cooking thus are Mediterranean, with a naturally attendant abundance of fresh vegetable type things with bright colors. And herbs.

By contrast, all other Southern cooking has its roots in southern British cooking, which has its own roots in older German and Danish tribal fare (Saxons and Angles). Typical southern "home-cooking" restaurant menus will have more in common with the Czech food I grew up with than with Italian or French food. At any rate, the heritage of non-Cajun Southern cooking, hailing from Germany, would explain the similarities between home cooking in the South and home cooking in central Europe—heavy sauces, heavy on the meat and dumplings and bread, lots of frying. The problem with Southern food, as you've probably heard about German food, is that after eating it you're hungry again in 72 hours.

We're most famous for barbecue, of course. For those of you unfamiliar with the verb "barbecue" used as a noun, when we say "barbecue" we mean "barbecued meat." I remember being in the third grade, fairly new to the deep south, and hearing someone speak of "great barbecue." I asked, "barbecued what?" He replied, "barbecue!" He didn't grasp our linguistic stumbling block, but I learned that "barbecue" is a noun in the South. If a Southerner refers to "barbecue" without further specification, he means pork. If you say "barbeque" in any restaurant outside Texas, we'll bring you shredded pork (usually shoulder), either swimming in sauce, or with tons of sauce on the side. There will always be a bottle of store-bought hot sauce nearby.

Outside barbecue, our most famous dishes are greens, black-eyed peas, and cornbread. And you can make plain old mustard, collard, or turnip greens a delicacy: Cook with white wine vinegar, honey or sugar, salt, hot sauce, bacon, and onions. You can tweak black-eyed peas and cornbread just as nicely with a little imagination.

As far as actual cooking techniques (as Alton Brown puts it, cooking is the application of heat to food) and barbecue, there's pretty much just fire, smoke, and meat, as discussed earlier. Our second most famous technique is deep frying. Bread it and deep fry it, and you'll find a Southerner who'll eat it. Just recently, I did it to orange roughy filets, but we do it to green tomato slices, okra, zucchini, pickles, and as I mentioned, a steak. Pop-tarts is about the only thing we won't deep fry, but don't quote me on that. I might be among the first to do it. Deep frying does wonderful things to food that other cooking methods don't do.

The other techniques we've either created or adopted include throwing a ham hock in it; splashing Tabasco in it; putting gravy on it; wrapping biscuits around it; cooking it in lard and/or bacon; and church socializing around it ("Baptist" is next to "pot luck" in the dictionary). Each of these techniques was developed to keep Southerners happy and full. The heart-healthers, animal-firsters, nouvelle-cuisiners, and similar ilks of folks might not be happy with Southern cooking, but we'd still be happy to offer them a plate of biscuits with ham and redeye gravy. A heads-up: We've heard the "I'll have a grit" jokes.

7

What to Do About It

THE PROBLEM

By now, our explorations of food have demonstrated that the ways in which government interferes in your daily life would take thousands of pages to list in any detail. Regulations, taxes, and licensing at every step of production of every good and service—not just food—burden us by nearly doubling the cost of everything on the market.

Add to this the opportunity cost: the wealth that *could* have been produced by all those people and departments of corporations whose entire jobs are made up of ensuring that government regulations are obeyed. And this excludes such things as welfare, the court system, and everything else government does inefficiently. Thomas Sowell, the Hoover Institute economist, has said it so often in his syndicated column that the number is burned into my long-term memory: Up to 65% of the money government takes from us for social-service programs is lost to bureaucratic overhead.

What that means in real terms is that you produce wealth by working at your job; you hold that wealth as a readily exchangeable store of value (money); and you then use that money to buy the wealth other people produce, in the form of products or services. By going into the market with your money, you stimulate other people to produce. By rewarding the good producers (e.g., Honda), and punishing the bad ones (e.g., DeSoto), your purchasing decisions tell producers when they're doing well and when they're not. You thus decide which producers survive, and which don't.

The government takes much of this incentive for production—this money—away, by simply taking it out of the market and paying government employees to do paperwork that does *not* result in any wealth being produced. The end result is that our standard of living is much lower than it could be. This is guaranteed to continue. Government destruction of wealth works in many ways, but the most obvious and costly is that millions of government employees taking a salary from the market, but not producing anything, means many potentially productive people are being wasted, and are to that extent acting as parasites on the economy. Remember, that refers only to *their* productivity. Add to that the effect of their drain on *your* productivity.

Additionally, high taxation and regulation serve directly as disincentives to our most productive individuals. As just one example, I know a successful cardio-thoracic surgeon who is closing his private practice and moving into medical consulting because the government, and insurers operating with the government's blessing, tell the surgeon how much he can charge for his services. Often the allowable fees are below the surgeon's cost. His case is indeed representative of a trend: Since the prices we pay for medical care are rising, you'd think the medical field would attract more newcomers, as the computer field has since the 1980s. Instead, applications to attend medical schools are decreasing across the country. Promising young talents are becoming lawyers instead.

There are other ways government threatens you. The Environmental Protection Agency, for example, raises the cost of owning land by stealing property without invoking imminent domain and without compensating the property owner. The EPA does this by declaring that you can't develop land you already own. The typical example involves someone buying beachfront property to build a home, only to have the EPA declare that some endangered species is threatened by development of your property. Suddenly, the property you saved for years to purchase is worthless. Be careful about buying rural land in the US—this can happen to you.

Federal government isn't the only threat: *Local* government, in numerous documented cases, has condemned land merely so they can give it to developers whose projects might expand the tax base, thus increasing the local government's income. These cases aren't the typical public-good cases, where a road is being built. Rather, local governments are condemning homeowners' property to build shopping malls that could just as easily be built somewhere else—the most recent case, in late 2003, arose in Alabaster, Alabama.[1] City Council members are choosing between one private party and another to decide who gets the land—never mind that one private party already had a home there.

Government boils down to a group of individuals no wiser than you or me who have the legal power to use force to do and to get what they want. They can

---

1.   See a report at http://www.shelbycountyreporter.com/articles/2003/09/10/news/news04.txt, accessed May 2004.

force you to do what they want—force you to give them everything you have that they want to take.

Imagine how much better things would be if the federal government merely obeyed the constitution, and limited its activity to coining money, making sure the states play fair with each other in economic transactions, adjudicating disputes between states, managing national defense, and representing the states in relations with foreign governments. If the federal government had kept itself to these responsibilities the last 200 years, we wouldn't have the problems we have with it today. Walter Williams, the famous economist at George Mason University, estimates that 75% of the federal government's budget is unconstitutional.

Look what the federal government has usurped over just the last 100 years:

It has forcibly taken over our retirement savings by taking money from us and giving it to some retired people today, on the promise that there will be money to take from others and give to us when we get older. (You don't have a Social Security savings account in your name—that trust fund has been raided perennially by our representatives in Congress.)

The federal government has put itself in charge of pollution over our entire land. Instead of private property owners being able to sue directly anyone who pollutes their land, the EPA and federal judges allow electricity plants in West Virginia to kill fish on private property in New York. If the polluter is within EPA regulations, and a federal judge decides the public good is served by allowing the polluter to continue, you lose your lawsuit and your fish. You are without recourse.[2]

And, as we've seen, the federal government intrudes into what should be private relationships between food producers and their employees and customers. The Constitution doesn't allow for any of it. That's what got me started on this book.

Why doesn't it work out well when government manages all these things? There are a thousand reasons, but here are two of the biggest:

---

2. For more discussion, see my article here: http://www.mises.org/fullarticle. asp?control=1371&id=68, and see examples of lawsuits here: http://www. zerowasteamerica.org/NYsuesEPA.htm and here: http://www.osti. gov/energycitations/product.biblio.jsp?osti_id=7032511, accessed May, 2004.

Lack of Market Discipline

When you sell food, build cars, manufacture shoes, give massages, or make or do anything to attract customers, those customers must leave the transaction convinced that they are better off than they were before they did business with you. They must feel that they'd rather have your restaurant meal than the $50 they paid for it; that they'd rather have that BMW 760i than the $110,000 they paid for it. Otherwise, they won't come back, word will get around, and you'll be out of business.

Government agencies and departments are not subject to this discipline. If the thing they're providing—education, for example—is inferior, rather than going bankrupt and letting competitors do it better, government only takes more of your money. Those taking the money always will claim that *this* budget infusion will fix things (even though the previous umpteen budget infusions resulted in the government service only getting worse).

A corollary of this is that there can be no accounting for what the cost of the services government provides really should be. There is accounting for the cost of building houses: If you are a homebuilder, and your houses cost more than every other homebuilder's houses because your employees are lazy or your suppliers are gouging you, you'll be out of business soon. The market values your houses however it will, so to survive you find that you must count the pennies that go into the production of those houses, and cut costs wherever you can. You have to be aware that the market also keeps track of quality, so if you cut costs in the wrong way (using inferior materials rather than training your employees to work more efficiently), you go out of business over that, too.

With government, there is no such accounting. Since government forcibly prevents competition for the provision of most of its services, government has no idea how much the market values its product—how much people are really willing to pay, and how much the service would cost if it were provided by a firm subject to the rigors of market competition.

The government can never go bankrupt. It needs only to tax you some more if it needs more money. And the more its efforts fail, the more it will claim to need more money. To see this at work, think about whether your local sales taxes are higher, or lower, than they were 20 years ago. The same goes for gasoline taxes, though most of us don't even know what we're paying in gasoline taxes. It's a self-perpetuating circle: The more free money the government gets from you, the more inefficient it becomes, and the worse its service becomes, justifying its demand for increasing taxes, and so on, and so on...

That's where accounting for the cost of government operations becomes insid-ious: You drive on public roads, and you pay for them through your gasoline taxes, but you don't know exactly how much of your income went into the roads you drove on last year (nor how much of your money went into roads you didn't use). You also don't know how much you paid for your neighbor's children to attend government schools last year. Uncovering the true dollar amounts we each pay for government services would take more time than any of us could afford. You paid, though, even if you don't have children of your own.

Lack of Proper Individual Incentives

So much for the "pressures" facing government agencies. As for individuals, when you and I toil at our jobs in the private sector, we know we have to do good work, or we can be fired. This may be less true for corporate employees than for small business owners (who can be fired by the market at any time, without warning, if the market just stops buying the product); but it is far less true for government employees than for everyone else.

The market—that's you and me, buying and selling as we wish, doing what's in our own best interest—is the final arbiter of quality and desirability. (It is true that great advertising can overcome quality or price problems, but only in the short run—only until word of mouth bankrupts the producer who has quality, price, or even internal accounting problems. Remember the Chevy Vega, or more recently, EMachines and Enron.)

Government employees—especially political appointees and elected offi-cials—don't have to do right by their customers (you and me) to keep their jobs. When public schools and their teachers produce illiterate high-school graduates, we don't fire the teachers and administrators. Instead, we often vote to let them take more of our money!

Government judges can hand down one insane decision after another without consequence. When successful appeals show a court's decisions to be wrong-headed time and time again, the wrongheaded judges don't lose their jobs or face any kind of disciplinary action. No policemen ever lose their jobs (and few chiefs of police) when the crime rate in their city creeps upward year after year. If this were to happen on the watch of a private security provider, by contrast, that secu-rity provider would find himself unemployed. City policemen only get more tax money when they're ineffective.

A final, awful aspect of the incentives individual government employees face is this: Bureaucrats who are responsible for signing off on budgets usually have *inef-*

ficiency as their primary goal. If a government department goes under budget during a given period, its budget may be cut the next period. If the same department spends more than it was allotted, or runs out of money early, it is given more money the next year.

This is the opposite of how it works in the market, where profitability is largely a function of efficiency. In private businesses, serving customers who enter transactions voluntarily is rewarded, and the better the customers are served, and the lower the costs in serving them (lower costs usually mean lower prices for you and me, remember), the greater the rewards for the businessman. To distill that thought: The *better* the public is served, the better the individual businessman fares. For government employees, it works in the opposite way.

This all assumes government people are honest and hard-working. (Think about that—our government will continue to do less with more *even if* everybody in government puts forth a sincere effort!) It gets even worse when there is real corruption in government. Remember the Enron bankruptcy. Enron's self-generated problems got as bad as they did because government shirked the very oversight duties it usurped from the market, in exchange for campaign contributions to congressmen and senators.[3] The federal government even gave Enron huge grants to do business—free money.

It was the market that first recognized the problems with Enron. The plummeting stock price alerted the government that there was a problem that couldn't be ignored. And of course, it's only the Enron executives who faced legal trouble; no congressman or senator who enabled them was threatened in any way. Individual congressmen, to the contrary, had the incentive all along to turn a blind eye to Enron's peccadilloes in exchange for continuing campaign and party contributions.

At bottom, the effects of government's interference in the market are as multifaceted as they are immense. This owes in large part to the distorted incentives individuals face when their job security rests on the fact that they can legally use the coercive force of government to get what they want. It will ever be so; that is the nature of government.

The direct cost of government is about half of everything you and I earn. The indirect costs may be even greater: Without government's involvement, what

---

3.   For documentation of my statements regarding Enron, do a web search using the terms "Enron government's fault," "Enron campaign contributions," and "Enron Congressional testimony" for more documentation than you can shake a Congressman at.

could our productivity be? How much how much less expensive, safer, and more varied our food supply?

THE SOLUTION

It's not going to be easy to get government off our backs and out of our kitchens. Government is huge. Even your city government, even if you live in a small town, is too big for any of us to handle alone. But we can win—we can scale government back at least to the size envisioned by the founders, and reclaim at least some of our liberty. It's a lot of work; we have to be persistent; many of us have to work together; and we have to be satisfied with small victories, though not so satisfied that we rest on our laurels. As the founders said, liberty requires constant vigilance.

What to do?

Become a Lobbyist

First, vote for those politicians who promise to reduce the size and scope of government. Often, this means voting libertarian,[4] though this is not a permanent solution—anybody who takes political office is at risk of becoming power-drunk. The problem is the power and lack of accountability that office holders enjoy. I enjoyed a tiny sampling of it while at the CIA, and even though my taste of it was on a microscopic scale, power without accountability has a predictable effect on anyone—even Thomas Jefferson.

Once people are in office, libertarian or not, hold their feet to the fire constantly: Pressure them to eliminate programs, cut budgets for the programs they don't eliminate, and vote against every new law that is not strictly constitutional, along with nearly every new law that *is* strictly constitutional. Encourage them to work toward the elimination of their very offices.

---

4.   Yes, there are libertarians who merely want legalized drugs, prostitution, abortion, pornography, etc. More philosophical types sometimes call these "libertine libertarians." Indeed, the libertines are correct that the government has no business telling you what you can put into your own body. Fortunately, most libertarians are libertarians not because they want to get high, but because they understand the founding of our country and the notion of natural rights. Your local Libertarian Party chapter is probably made up mostly of the latter sort.

This is not as impractical as you think. There are office holders around the nation who wish to scale back government. Congressman Ron Paul (R-TX) is probably the best-known example.[5] While he is officially a Republican, he votes against every bill in Congress that is not consistent with the Constitution. He votes against interventions overseas, in favor of free trade, and against government fiddling with business and with the money supply. These positions are all consistent with the Constitution and with the vision of the founders.

Now—how exactly can you apply pressure to the people who are in office today? After all, we must deal with the present crop of incumbents first. The best way, it appears, is to write letters. Office holders, for whatever reason, are more impressed with snail mail than with e-mails or telephone calls. Keep your letters short, to the point, and reasonable. Don't use huge words and complicated arguments they won't understand (their staffers read and screen them anyway), and don't do any ranting.

Just tell your representative how to vote or act on whatever issue you're discussing, and include a short explanation of why—just a few sentences. Do this often, and do it to everyone who governs the place where you live. This means your mayor, any elected local and state judges and law enforcement officers, your state legislators, and the people in Washington who govern you, which includes congressmen, senators, and the president.

In the days of email, snail mail is time-consuming, annoying, and requires you to buy government stamps,[6] but it's worth the effort. While most office holders don't actually read much of the mail addressed to them, they do request reports from their staffers about the mail they're getting. The more reasoned, concise, and literate your letter is, the more memorable it will be, and the better chance it will have of being read by the person to whom you addressed it.

Home School

The most effective, most important thing you can do for the long term is to home school your children and persuade everyone you know to home school theirs. Much of what government schools teach is unquestioning obedience to the government. In my own school upbringing, this began every morning when

---

5.   Read about Ron Paul at his House website, http://www.house.gov/paul/, and read his writings and speeches on his archive at http://www.lewrockwell.com/paul/paul-arch.html.

6.   Government enforces a monopoly on first-class mail delivery, too. Note how much better Fedex and UPS handle overnight delivery than does the USPS.

the first thing we did was recite the pledge of allegiance. (Needless to say, pledging allegiance to your government is the opposite of what the founders did—they overthrew the government they grew up with.)

It has long been established that home-schooled children are academically far ahead of both their public-school peers and most private-schooled children. The newest data show that home-schooled children are even better socialized, which negates the only argument the government schoolteachers had to oppose home schooling.[7]

If you home school your children, they are vastly more likely to end up competent, confident, and independent as adults (not to mention healthy). Plus, you have absolute control over what your children are taught, and you have *much* more incentive for your children to do well than do public schoolteachers. Investigate the option of neighborhood schools as well, such as cooperative schools where several professional parents take turns teaching different subjects. Keep in mind that one-room schoolhouses, where 6-year-olds and 16-year olds learned in the same room, provided better educations 100 years ago than public, and even private, schools do today.

As more people in the US home school, more of tomorrow's business and community leaders will understand the meaning and purpose of liberty and the inherent danger of a government that continually improvises its own rules. The payoff, in the long term, will be increased liberty and a government that realizes it should be a *servant* of the people if it is to exist at all. This is what our nation's founders had in mind, as the Declaration of Independence makes explicit. It is proper that elected officials should constantly fear impeachments and recalls, and entire agencies should fear being abolished. That's how the market already treats the rest of us, and it's what helps us keep our focus on the customers we serve.

Legally Avoid Taxes

This seems like a small matter at first, but you can reduce the taxes you pay to support the government by buying things secondhand. Secondhand home schooling curricula are available on the web and most likely in your city. Estate sales occasionally offer up-market quality at a reasonable, sometimes rock-bottom

---

7.   Indeed, this has been known to researchers since the mid-1980s. See a review at http://www.ericfacility.net/ericdigests/ed372460.html, and do a web search for the term "home schooling socialization" to see how well the home-schooled fare into adulthood.

price, and usually include furniture, books, appliances, tools, and clothing. Anything you can get at estate and garage sales helps keep the government out of your pocket.

You can already read classic literature, the best (and worst) political and economic commentary, and mountains of historical and legal documents on the web for free. Maps, how-to guides, recipes…there's very little in print that isn't on the Internet now. Real books, printed on paper, will always have a market, as it will always be nice to have a book to carry around for any single document that requires more than an hour or so to read. But using the Internet as much as it's comfortable means you pay taxes only on that service. The fewer documents you have to purchase new, the less tax you pay.

You can buy vegetables at farmer's markets rather than at your local megamart. You may not avoid local sales taxes that way, but you'd avoid some federal taxation. For example, when you buy national brands at a mega-mart, the national brands and the mega-mart pay Social Security, Medicare/Medicaid, and federal unemployment insurance on behalf of their employees. That cost is passed on to you.

You can also buy from folks selling out of the back of a truck on the side of a country road. Always take a look at their offerings: The fruits and vegetables may be fresher, may be truly vine-ripened (therefore more flavorful and slightly more nutritious), and you avoid sales taxes.

It is possible that a roadside hawker will lie to you about whether he grows his own vegetables, as he could be getting them from the same distributor that supplies your local large grocery store, but consider this: If the guy in the truck got his vegetables from a big distributor, but he sells them for a lower price than at your local grocery store, then you're better off buying from the truck (and not paying sales taxes). If he grew them himself, then you're getting superior vegetables for less. As long as his prices are lower, you win. If his prices are higher than your grocer's, then you'd have to judge the quality of the vegetables more carefully.

Finally, try growing your own vegetables, as discussed earlier. But you can take that idea a step farther: Persuade your neighbors to grow their own as well. One option is for each family to specialize in one vegetable, and grow as much of it as possible. Then everyone trades with everyone else in the neighborhood. You'll be thrilled with the results—trust me. Not only will everyone end up with tons of free food, but everyone will know, trust, and enjoy each other better as neighbors. It's my suspicion that this sort of sense of community provided much of the courage our founders showed in facing up to their own government in 1776.

Own Guns

If you don't have one, consider buying a gun. This doesn't mean you're some kind of kook or militant militia survivalist (nor does it mean that militia members are necessarily radicals, as they've been unfairly portrayed by the mass media).

Learn how to use the gun(s) by getting some instruction, preferably before you buy any. If you have children in the house, be aware that Mel Gibson, the actor of *Mad Max* and *Passion of Christ* fame, is only one example of millions of parents who have taught their children shooting safety and skills. Home handgun accidents involving children are so infrequent in the US as to be of infinitesimal significance compared to the dangers of wading pools and bathtubs, which kill *far* more children than guns, regardless what the Clintons claimed (Bill's mid-1990s claim regarding the number of children killed included "children" up to age 24, and included gang violence).[8] To bring the point home: How many children do you know of who have either accidentally or deliberately stabbed each other with kitchen knives or forks, items they have access to every day?

There are multiple benefits to having a gun in the home: First, you can defend yourself from ordinary criminals. Crime drops when more citizens like yourself own guns. Remember that when a criminal breaks into your house, he's not going to wait for you to dial 911, and he's not going to wait for the police to show up 15 to 30 minutes later. The mere sound of you chambering a round in a pump shotgun is enough to send 99.9% of criminals running back out the way they came in. For that .01% of criminals who don't run, perhaps stoned on speed or cocaine, your shooting them with the shotgun will stop them when their own instinct for self-preservation won't.

The second reason to own guns is to protect yourself from your government. This is the most important reason to own guns, and the real reason the 2nd amendment was added to the Constitution. The *Federalist Papers*, and federal court cases following the constitutional amendment emancipating the slaves, made it clear that gun ownership is the first test of whether a population is truly

---

8.   See John Lott's archive at LewRockwell.com: http://www.lewrockwell.com/lott/lott-arch.html. Lott is the author of *More Guns, Less Crime*, the best-seller in which he analyzed literally all extant gun crime statistics in the US covering the last century.

free.[9] Free people are armed and able to resist a totalitarian government. Unarmed people are subjugated people.

If you don't believe an armed populace is enough to fend off the US government, just consider: With the populace being armed, the military can never be big enough to dominate, as domination requires occupation—by soldiers on foot. At the same time, read up on Ruby Ridge and Waco if you don't believe our government is capable of taking up arms against its citizens, and being wrong on the particulars when doing so.

The final thing guns do is protect you from foreign invasion. No government has ever attempted to invade and occupy the US, and no government ever will as long as more than 80 million and more of us are armed. Even in WWII, Japan didn't want to invade our mainland because, as their Admiral Isoroku Yamamoto said, "You cannot invade the mainland United States. There would be a rifle behind each blade of grass." Remember also the World Trade Center attacks: Those were possible only because law-abiding citizens and *pilots* were prohibited from carryings guns on planes. We were allowed to carry guns on planes until the 1960s.

Spread the Word

The last thing you can do, but certainly not the least, is to inform yourself and persuade others. We don't need government in charge of the food supply, in charge of automobile safety, or in charge of our retirement savings. Learn for yourself, by reading history and political analysis. Three of the most important names you should familiarize yourself with are Lysander Spooner, Murray Rothbard, and Ludwig von Mises. You can find most of what each of them wrote for free on the Internet. You are the most effective agent for change, and only you can contribute to a safer, healthier, more peaceful, wealthier, and happier future for your children and grandchildren.

There are hundreds, perhaps thousands of groups you can join, from your local or regional Libertarian Party chapter to a chapter of the Federalist Society. You can even start your own organization, and watch it grow. The Internet is making it easier all the time, and is bringing together those of us with an understanding of liberty and of our own country's early days. You can start your own

---

9.   See, for example, http://www.davekopel.com/2A/LawRev/35FinalPartOne.htm, and http://www.old-yankee.com/rkba/racial_laws.html, both accessible as of May 2004.

email discussion list, or join existing lists, on Yahoo! and other Internet sites. The possibilities for spreading the word about liberty are limited only by your imagination.

Conclusion

So now you know what government is doing in your soup, and I hope you have some ideas you didn't have before regarding what can be done about it. I also hope you're persuaded that our lives would be improved with a reduction of government interference, and that you're motivated to take action.

Any action at all is good, even if it amounts to mailing only one letter to one elected official. Keep in mind, though, that reducing government is similar to improving your health—one healthy meal, or one exercise session, is good, but for real change to take place, you have to make a lifestyle change. Fortunately, as we've seen, you can make lifestyle changes with regard to food that not only will improve your physical condition, but will forever make government a smaller part of your daily life.

If this sounds like a lot of work, well, it is. Anything truly good is hard work, as sources from the Bible to Mark Twain have already told us, and as you've learned the hard way if you've tried to be a real expert in your career field. Liberty is no exception, but frankly, liberty is more important in the long run than whatever you're doing for a living now. That doesn't mean you can afford to quit work, blow your savings, and starve your family, but it does mean that making changes, such as home schooling or starting a garden or even a neighborhood garden co-op, are worth the trouble.

Do I believe government will be scaled back, after more than two centuries of American history when it has only gotten bigger and more intrusive? Yes! Remember that JFK and Reagan were able to cut personal income taxes. Remember that during WWII, food was rationed, but that disgusting practice stopped after the war.

However, other things instituted during WWII that were supposed to be temporary, such as federal income taxes being withheld from your paycheck, have proven permanent. Almost every "temporary" government intrusion becomes permanent. Bureaucrats and elected officials *never* have a personal interest in seeing government scaled back.

But I believe it will happen. As George W. Bush, a champion of expanding government,[1] said himself in a December 2003 public appearance, "There's something in the American character that always looks for a better way and is unimpressed when others say it cannot be done." In this statement, Bush is correct. Americans, particularly with the help of the blossoming and to date unregulated Internet, finally have access to everything they need to find ways to scale back government: access to information about government interventions and how they hamper progress; access to merchants around the country and the world who can send us new, better, sometimes exotic food products at lower prices (at least whenever our prying government allows the products to cross borders); and instant communication with people of like minds.

And your kitchen will always be the first, most effective, and most enjoyable place to declare your personal sovereignty. Let's get to work!

---

1.   You can check a number of government and private websites for the most up-to-date spending data, and you'll find that Bush II has increased spending faster than anyone since (and possibly including) LBJ. For one summary and commentary, see http:// www.thenewamerican.com/tna/2002/09-09-2002/vol8no18_disguise_print.htm, accessed May 2004.

0-595-31816-9